A wooden sailing ship on the Nile.
Un voilier en bois sur le Nil.
Ein Segelschiff aus Holz auf dem Nil.
(Asuan, 1959)

NICOLAAS BIEGMAN

EGYPT'S SIDE-SHOWS

LES À-CÔTÉS DE L'EGYPTE ÄGYPTISCHE IMPRESSIONEN

THAMES AND HUDSON

Dedicated to Mustafa, the best driver in Egypt, who was present while
a number of these photographs were being taken.

Dédicacé à Mustafa, le meilleur chauffeur de l'Egypte, qui assistait à la prise
de vue d'un nombre de ces photographies.

Mustafa gewidmet, dem besten Fahrer von Ägypten, der dabei war,
als eine Anzahl dieser Photographien aufgenommen wurde.

Painting on a pilgrim's house
Peinture sur la maison d'un pèlerin
Malerei auf den Haus eines Pilgers
(Qaransho, 1966)

My beloved Egypt, where I spent seven and a half years of my life – a month in 1959; three years from 1964 to 1967; almost four and a half years from 1984 to 1988; and a week in 1990 – is more than many other countries blessed with maturity. It has not been invented or created in a region freshly discovered or emptied of its inhabitants. It has not been laid out according to a master plan. It has, as far as memory stretches, always been there. It has had the opportunity to grow in a natural manner.

At this point, someone might say it has grown too quickly. He would be right, especially with regard to the present century. Egypt, the inhabitable three per cent of which is exactly as big as the Netherlands, counted less than ten million people around 1900 and has reached well over fifty-five million since. Every eight to nine months a million is added to its population. A rather low standard of living is the only reason why the country has not yet literally exploded with people: Egyptians take up less space with their housing and transport requirements than most Europeans or Americans. Conversely, the high birth rate is largely rooted in the low standard of living. How many people will Egypt eventually be able to hold? One hundred million? It will reach that stage by 2020. Two hundred? Thirty years later.

Over the last five years the government's population policy has grown more vigorous, and the trend seems to be on the point of being reversed. Even if that happens, stabilization will not occur at less than 110 million, which is still a formidable number.

However, this book is not concerned with Egypt's many problems or with its uncertain future, nor does it deal with its famous stone monuments. The statues, temples, obelisks and pyramids are a source of inspiration for many visitors, and a source of foreign currency for the country. They belong to the most beautiful and impressive products of humanity. They have been painted, drawn and photographed innumerable times and are reproduced in a number of splendid publications. The same applies to the idyllic, vanishing Egyptian countryside, with its camels, donkeys and buffalo.

This book includes more of the commonplace than the spectacular. It deals with subjects encountered by chance, which drew my attention because of any of a variety of aspects: sadness, exhilaration – Egypt possesses extraordinary amounts of both – originality, and sometimes a feeling I had with regard to Egypt as a whole: that I had seen it just in time. Many of the photographs reproduced here are directly or indirectly related to religion. Religion is an omnipresent phenomenon in Egypt. Everyone belongs to a religion, whether as a Muslim, a Christian or, sometimes, a Jew. Atheism, though frequently encountered in other parts of the world, is almost nonexistent in Egypt, and socially unacceptable. God is everywhere.

Long ago, and only for a few centuries, Egypt was a Christian country. The seventh century A.D. saw the Arab Muslim conquest. During the following centuries, approximately ninety per cent of the population converted to Islam, and everyone traded in the Coptic language for Arabic.

The 'Copts', the remaining five million Christians, cannot be distinguished at first sight from their Muslim compatriots. They share the same way of life, even though there are differences in certain customs: for instance, tattooing is done only at Christian festivities – most Copts have a cross tattooed on their wrist – but the tattooers themselves are Muslims.

God brings sorrow as well as joy. Still, many Egyptians prefer to attribute their bad luck to the Evil Eye, the gaze of envy, which, as the people say, can split stones. Protection against the Evil Eye is derived from amulets *(higab)*, which come in the shape of an eye, mostly blue, the hand of Fatima with the five fingers *(khamsa wa-khmaysa)*, the number 5 referring to those fingers, or some or all of them combined with a formula such as 'God is most great' *(Allahu akbar)*, or *ya nas ya sharr kifaya arr:* 'People, Evil, stop your envious prattle!'

Many Egyptians, both Muslim and Christian, feel that in their contact with God they need the mediation or intercession *(tawassut* or *shafa'a)* of a saint, alive or, more often, dead. The tombs of the saints are marked with a dome. If the saint is considered important, an annual pilgrimage or *moulid* is made to the tomb, where the saint's blessing *(baraka)* can be obtained; where, in the case of Muslim *moulids*, groups of dervishes perform their mystic dances *(zikr)*; and where there is trade and amusement. There are thousands of saints in Egypt, and new ones are added regularly. There are also thousands of *moulids*, big ones drawing over a million visitors and smaller ones attracting several hundred or more.

The pilgrimage to Mecca, the *hagg*, is an obligation which every Muslim who is financially and physically able to undertake it must perform at least once in his or her lifetime. With the progressive growth in affluence and the improvement of transportation, the numbers of pilgrims are increasing. In 1990, a comparatively slack year, there was a total of one and a half million pilgrims, among whom were 73,000 Egyptians flown in by Egypt Air to Jeddah from the airports of Cairo, Alexandria and Luxor. For the individual *hāgg* or *hāgga* (pilgrim) and for their relatives, friends and neighbours, the pilgrimage is as important as ever. The *hāggs* are a source of pride to their village, and they receive a boisterous welcome upon their return from the holy places.

During the absence of a pilgrim, the walls of his or her house are painted with pictures of holy places visited (the Ka'ba in Mecca, the Prophet's tomb in Medina), transport, real or imagined (airplane, train, boat, bus, camel), and whatever else the painter may have associated with the journey: police and customs officers, strange animals, birds, flowers, palm trees, or Buraq, the horse that carried the Prophet from Jerusalem to Heaven. In addition a number of edifying phrases are taken from the Koran and elsewhere, especially '*hagg* performed, sins forgiven' and 'the Prophet has said: "Whoever visits my tomb is entitled to my intercession."'

Such decorated houses are to be found everywhere in Egypt, but there are great differences in the exuberance and quality of the paintings. The appearance of an entire village is sometimes determined by the imagination and the technique of a single painter. Such is the case in Silwa Bahari, situated on the east bank of the Nile between Edfu and Asuan, where 'Id Yasin 'Ali has embellished the houses on both sides of the main street. Likewise, 'Ali Sayyid has left his mark on Ballas/Al-Mahrousa, not far from Qena. In Fayoum as well, villages are distinguished by their painted homes. Unfortunately, the paintings on the outer walls are at the mercy of sun, wind, dust and rain, rare though the rain may be, and are certainly not blessed with eternal life. After a few years, they begin to lose their colours, and after another few, they disappear altogether. But in the meantime, other paintings have been made on other houses.

A number of photographs show deserts and oases. The Nile Valley and the Delta, where the great majority of Egyptians live, are surrounded by extensive deserts; flat and sandy in the north and west, mountainous along the Red Sea. In fact, the inhabited area is one large oasis. In the Libyan desert, west of the Nile, there are a number of smaller oases: Bahariya, Farafra, Dakhla and Kharga, and near the Libyan border lies Siwa, where a Berber language is spoken. In Siwa and Kharga there are Pharaonic temples.

Along the western shores of the Red Sea there are several places where water is found. This is the home of the 'Ababda and the Bisharin, non-Arabic-speaking peoples related to the Hadendoa and others living in the coastal mountains and plains of Sudan and Eritrea. In this area there are also remnants from antiquity: granite quarries, Roman watch towers, camps and settlements.

In the Sinai desert there are oases along the coasts of the Mediterranean, the Gulf of Suez and the Gulf of 'Aqaba and inland.

The higher mountains usually consist of granite, the lower hills of Nubian sandstone. In the oasis of Farafra there are white formations reminiscent of icebergs.

Most of the photographs do not, I think, require much introduction. There are images of ships, tombs, fish, old cars, inscriptions and various buildings.

Foremost, the reader will encounter many Egyptians. After all, the Egyptians make up the most characteristic and attractive aspect of their country. It is thanks to them that Cairo, 'the mother of the world' with its thirteen, fourteen or fifteen million citizens, is not only one of the safest but also one of the most amusing cities on earth. They are hospitable, warm and tolerant and they have an inexhaustible sense of humour. I hope they will keep these characteristics for a long time to come. In more ways than one, they still have much to teach us.

Jubbega, 23 June 1991

Mon Egypte bien-aimée, où j'ai passé sept ans et demi de ma vie - un mois en 1959, trois ans de 1964 à 1967, presque quatre ans et demi de 1984 à 1988 et une semaine en 1990 - est plus que nombre d'autres pays dotée de maturité. Elle n'a pas été inventée ou créée dans une région nouvellement découverte ou vidée de ses habitants. Elle n'a pas été aménagée selon un plan général. De mémoire d'homme elle a été là. Elle a eu l'opportunité de se développer de façon naturelle.

Et de se développer beaucoup trop vite, dirait quelqu'un peut-être ici. Il aurait raison, surtout en ce qui concerne le siècle en cours. L'Egypte, dont les trois pour cent qui sont habitables ont exactement les mêmes dimensions que les Pays-Bas, comptait moins de dix millions d'habitants vers 1900 et en a maintenant près de soixante. Tous les huit à neuf mois leur nombre augmente d'un million. Le niveau de vie assez peu élevé est la seule raison pour laquelle le pays n'a pas encore littéralement explosé: les Egyptiens occupent moins d'espace avec leurs besoins d'habitation et de voyage que la plupart des Européens ou des Américains. Contrairement, une grande partie de la fécondité prend racine dans le bas niveau de vie. L'Egypte, combien d'habitants pourrait-elle éventuellement contenir? Cent millions? Ce niveau sera atteint vers 2020. Deux cents millions? Ce sera trente ans après.

Au courant des cinq dernières années la politique démographique du gouvernement est devenue plus ferme et tout porte à croire que la tendance est sur le point d'être renversée. Même si cela arrive la stabilisation ne se fera pas à un nombre inférieur à 110 millions, ce qui est toujours formidable.

Mais le présent livre ne veut pas aborder les nombreux problèmes de l'Egypte ou son avenir incertain. Il ne veut pas non plus parler des fameux monuments. Les statues, temples, obélisques et pyramides forment une source d'inspiration pour de nombreux visiteurs et une source de devises étrangères pour le pays. Ils comptent parmi les plus beaux et les plus impressionnants produits de l'humanité. Ils ont été peints, dessinés et photographiés des milliers de fois et figurent dans un grand nombre de splendides publications. Il en est de même pour la campagne égyptienne idyllique en voie de disparition avec ses chameaux, ses ânes et ses buffles. Dans ce livre il s'agit plus de l'ordinaire que du spectaculaire, de sujets rencontrés par hasard, qui m'ont frappé pour une variété de raisons: tristesse, joie - l'Egypte possède les deux en abondance -, originalité, singularité et parfois le même sentiment que j'avais pour l'Egypte

dans sa totalité: que j'ai été juste à temps pour la voir.

Beaucoup des illustrations recueillies dans ce livre se rapportent de manière directe ou indirecte à la religion. La religion est un phénomène omniprésent en Egypte. Tout le monde adhère à une religion, que ce soit comme musulman ou comme chrétien ou, parfois, comme juif. Quelque fréquent l'athéisme puisse être dans d'autres parties du monde, il n'existe pas en Egypte où il est socialement inacceptable. Dieu est partout.

Il y a longtemps, et pendant quelques siècles seulement, l'Egypte a été un pays chrétien. Au cours du septième siècle le pays est conquis par les arabes musulmans. Dans le courant des siècles suivants la population est islamisée pour environ quatre-vingt-dix pour cent et tout le monde a changé la langue copte pour l'arabe.

A première vue les Coptes, les cinq millions de chrétiens qui restent, ne peuvent pas être distingués de leurs compatriotes musulmans. Ils partagent leur manière de vivre, bien qu'il y ait des différences dans certaines coutumes: par exemple le tatouage ne se fait qu'aux fêtes chrétiennes - la plupart des Coptes ont une croix tatouée au poignet - mais les tatoueurs sont des musulmans.

Dieu apporte la tristesse tout comme la joie. Pourtant bien des Egyptiens préfèrent attribuer leur mauvaise fortune au Mauvais Œil, le regard fixe de l'envie qui, à ce que dit le peuple, peut fendre des pierres. La protection contre le Mauvais Œil est tirée d'amulettes *(higab)* qui peuvent avoir la forme d'un œil, le plus souvent bleu, de la main de Fatima aux cinq doigts *(khamsa wa-khmaysa)*, du nombre 5 faisant allusion à ces doigts, ou de quelques-uns de ceux-ci ou de tous ensemble en combinaison avec une formule comme 'Dieu est infiniment grand' *(Allahu akbar)*, ou *ya nas ya sharr kifaya arr*: 'Peuple, Malheur, arrêtez votre caquetage envieux!'

Beaucoup d'Egyptiens, musulmans de même que chrétiens, sentent que dans leurs rapports avec Dieu ils ont besoin de la médiation ou de l'intercession *(tawassut* ou *shafa'a)* d'un saint, vivant ou, plus souvent, mort. Les tombes des saints sont marquées d'un dôme. Si le saint passe pour important, on fait chaque année un pèlerinage ou *moulid* autour de la tombe où on peut obtenir les bénédictions *(baraka)* du saint, où, dans le cas de *moulid* musulmans, des groupes de derviches exécutent leurs danses mystiques *(zikr)* et où on fait du commerce et s'amuse. Il y a des milliers de saints en Egypte et de nouveaux saints y sont ajoutés régulièrement. Il y a aussi des milliers de *moulid*, des grands avec plus d'un million de visiteurs ou des petits avec quelques centaines de visiteurs.

Le pèlerinage à La Mecque, le *hagg*, est une obligation que chaque musulman qui en est financièrement et physiquement capable, doit faire au moins une fois dans sa vie. Avec la croissance progressive de la prospérité et le progrès des moyens de transport le nombre de pèlerins s'accroît - en 1990, une année avec un nombre relativement modeste, il y avait au total un million et demi de pèlerins, parmi lesquels 73 000 Egyptiens qui arrivaient par avion d'Egypt Air à Djedda à partir des aéroports du Caire, Alexandrie ou Louxor -, mais pour le *hāgg* ou la *hāgga* individuel et leurs parents, amis et voisins, le pèlerinage est aussi important que jamais. Les *hāgg* sont une source d'orgueil pour leur village et ils sont fougueusement reçus à leur retour des lieux saints.

Pendant l'absence du pèlerin les murs de sa maison sont peints d'illustrations des lieux saints visités - le Ka'ba de La Mecque, la tombe du Prophète à Médine -, du moyen de transport, vrai ou imaginé - avion, train, bateau, autobus, chameau - et de n'importe quel sujet le peintre aurait pu associer au voyage: policiers et douaniers, animaux, oiseaux et fleurs exotiques, palmiers, ou Buraq, le cheval qui portait le Prophète de Jérusalem aux Cieux. Elles sont accompagnées d'un nombre de phrases édifiantes prises dans le Coran ou ailleurs, surtout '*hagg* accompli, péchés pardonnés' et 'le Prophète a dit: "Tous ceux qui visitent ma tombe, peuvent revendiquer mon intercession."'

Des maisons ainsi décorées se rencontrent partout en Egypte. De grandes différences existent cependant dans l'exubérance et la qualité des peintures. L'apparence d'un village entier est parfois déterminée par l'imagination et le talent d'un seul peintre. C'est le cas de Silwa Bahari sur la rive est du Nil entre Edfu et Assuan où 'Id Yasin 'Ali a décoré les maisons des deux côtés de la rue principale. De la même manière 'Ali Sayyid a laissé ses traces sur Ballas/Al-Mahrousa, pas loin de Qena. Dans la région du Fayoum aussi les villages se distinguent par leurs maisons peintes. Malheureusement les peintures sur les murs extérieurs sont à la merci du soleil, des vents, de la poussière et de la pluie, quelque rare que la pluie y puisse être, et elles sont loin d'être éternelles. Après quelques années elles commencent à perdre leurs couleurs et encore quelques années et elles ont disparu. Mais en attendant d'autres peintures ont été faites sur d'autres maisons.

Certaines photographies se rapportent à des déserts et oasis. La vallée du Nil et le delta qui rassemblent la majeure partie des Egyptiens, sont entourés de déserts étendus, plats et sableux dans le nord et dans l'ouest, montagneux le long de la mer Rouge. En fait la surface habitée est une grande oasis. Le désert libyque, à l'ouest du Nil, contient un nombre de moins grandes oasis: Bahariya, Farafra, Dakhla et Kharga, et près de la frontière libyenne se trouve Siouah où on parle une langue berbère. Siouah et Kharga possèdent des temples pharaoniques.

Le long des côtes ouest de la mer Rouge il y a quelques endroits où on trouve de l'eau. C'est la région où habitent les 'Ababda et les Bisharin, peuples de langue non arabe apparentés aux Hadendoa et à d'autres peuples qui vivent dans les montagnes et plaines côtières du Soudan et de l'Erythrée. Ici aussi on trouve des restes de l'antiquité: carrières de granit, tours de guet, campements et implantations romains.

Dans le désert du Sinaï des oasis se rencontrent le long des côtes de la Méditerranée, du Golfe de Suez et du Golfe d''Aqaba de même que dans l'arrière-pays.

Les plus hautes montagnes se composent d'habitude de granit, les collines moins élevées de grès nubien. Dans l'oasis de Farafra des formations blanches font penser à des icebergs.

La plupart des photographies ne demandent pas beaucoup d'explication, à mon avis. Elles représentent des bateaux, des tombes, des poissons, des voitures anciennes, des inscriptions et différentes œuvres architecturales.

Mais le lecteur y trouvera surtout un assez grand nombre d'Egyptiens. Tout bien considéré ce sont les Egyptiens qui constituent les éléments les plus caractéristiques et les plus attrayants de leur pays. C'est grâce à eux que Le Caire, 'la mère du monde' avec ses treize, quatorze ou quinze millions d'habitants, n'est pas seulement une des villes les plus sûres, mais aussi des plus amusantes au monde. Ils sont hospitaliers, chaleureux et tolérants et ils ont un sens inépuisable de l'humour, dans les villes de même qu'à la campagne. J'espère qu'ils continueront longtemps encore à être tels qu'ils sont. A plus d'un égard ils ont encore beaucoup de choses à nous apprendre.

Jubbega, le 23 juin 1991

Mein geliebtes Ägypten, in dem ich insgesamt siebeneinhalb Jahre meines Lebens verbrachte - 1959 war ich einen Monat dort, 1964-67 drei Jahre, 1984-88 fast viereinhalb Jahre und 1990 eine Woche - ist mehr als viele andere Länder mit Reife gesegnet. Es wurde nicht in einer gerade erst entdeckten oder ihrer Ureinwohner beraubten Region erschaffen. Es wurde nicht nach einem Bauplan gestaltet; schon seit Menschengedenken existierte es einfach und wuchs auf natürliche Weise heran.

Wuchs viel zu schnell heran, könnte man einwenden und hätte damit in Bezug auf unser Jahrhundert sicher recht. Ägypten, dessen bewohnbare drei Prozent genau so groß sind wie das Territorium der Niederlande, zählte um 1900 weniger als zehn Millionen Einwohner. Heute sind es fast sechzig Millionen. Jeden achten oder neunten Monat kommt eine weitere Million dazu. Daß die Bevölkerungsexplosion das Land noch nicht gesprengt hat, liegt einzig und allein am niedrigen Lebensstandard: Ägypter brauchen viel weniger Platz zum Leben und stellen andere Anforderungen an Transport und Verkehr als Europäer und Amerikaner. Umgekehrt hat die hohe Geburtenrate ihren Grund in dem niedrigen Lebensstandard. Wie viele Millionen wird Ägypten letztendlich verkraften können? Hundert? Diese Zahl wird im Jahr 2020 erreicht sein. Dreißig Jahre später könnten es 200 Millionen sein.

Im Laufe der letzten fünf Jahre wurde die Bevölkerungspolitik der Regierung immer energischer, und die Tendenz scheint an einem Punkt der Umkehrung angelangt zu sein. Aber selbst wenn dies zutreffen sollte, wird eine Stabilisierung nicht eintreten bei weniger als 110 Millionen, was noch immer eine enorme Anzahl ist.

In diesem Buch geht es jedoch weder um Ägyptens zahlreiche Probleme, noch um seine unsichere Zukunft. Es handelt auch nicht von seinen berühmten Denkmälern aus Stein. Die Statuen, Tempel, Obelisken und Pyramiden sind für viele Besucher eine Quelle der Inspiration und bringen dem Land dringend benötigte Devisen. Sie zählen zu den schönsten und beeindruckendsten Schöpfungen der Menschheit. Man hat sie unzählige Male gezeichnet, fotografiert, gemalt und in hervorragenden Büchern veröffentlicht. Das gleiche gilt für die idyllische ägyptische Landschaft mit ihren Kamelen, Eseln und Büffeln, die im Verschwinden begriffen ist.

Dieses Buch bietet mehr Triviales als Spektakuläres. Es stellt eher zufällig entdeckte Aspekte dar, die aus verschiedenen Gründen meine Aufmerksamkeit erregt haben: Traurigkeit, Freude - Ägypten ist besonders reich an beiden -, Originalität, Skurrilität und manchmal eben dieses Gefühl, das ich für Ägypten als Ganzes habe: daß ich es gerade noch rechtzeitig erleben konnte. Viele meiner Fotos beschäftigen sich direkt oder indirekt mit Religion. Religion ist in Ägypten ein allgegenwärtiges Phänomen. Jeder gehört irgendeiner Religion an, sei es als Moslem, als Christ oder manchmal als Jude. Wie häufig der Atheismus in anderen Teilen der Welt vorkommen mag, in Ägypten ist er kaum verbreitet und gesellschaftlich verpönt. Gott ist überall.

Vor langer Zeit, allerdings nur ein paar Jahrhunderte lang, war Ägypten ein christliches Land. Im 7. Jahrhundert eroberten die Araber das Reich. Während der folgenden Jahrhunderte traten ungefähr neunzig Prozent der Bevölkerung zum Islam über, und man tauschte die koptische Sprache gegen die arabische aus.

Die 'Kopten', die fünf Millionen übrig gebliebenen Christen, unterscheiden sich auf den ersten Blick kaum von ihren moslemischen Landsleuten. Sie haben die gleiche Lebensweise, auch wenn einige Gebräuche unterschiedlich sind. Das Tätowieren zum Beispiel ist den christlichen Festen vorbehalten - die meisten Kopten haben sich ein Kreuz aufs Handgelenk tätowieren lassen -, wobei die Tätowierer jedoch Moslems sind.

Gott bringt sowohl Leid als auch Freude. Viele Ägypter schreiben ein Unglück aber lieber dem Bösen Auge zu, dem Blick des Neides, der, wie man sagt, Steine spalten kann. Schutz gegen das Böse Auge bieten Amulette *(higab)*, meistens in der Form eines blauen Auges, die Hand von Fatima mit den fünf Fingern *(khamsa wa-khmaysa)*, die Zahl 5, die sich auf diese Finger bezieht, oder einige bzw. alle von ihnen in Kombination mit einem Spruch wie 'Gott ist groß' *(Allahu akbar)* oder *ya nas ya sharr kifaya* arr: 'Menschen, Böse, hört auf mit eurem neidischen Geplapper.'

Viele Ägypter, Moslems und Christen, glauben, daß sie in ihrem Kontakt mit Gott Vermittlung oder Fürsprache brauchen *(tawassut oder shafa'a)*, und zwar in der Person eines lebendigen - öfter jedoch toten - Heiligen. Die Grabmäler der Heiligen erkennt man an einer Kuppel. Handelt es sich um einen wichtigen Heiligen, so findet eine jährliche Pilgerfahrt *(moulid)* um das Grab herum statt, wobei der Segen des Heiligen *(baraka)* empfangen werden kann, wo - im Falle von moslemischen *moulids* - Derwisch-Gruppen ihre mystischen Tänze *(zikr)* veranstalten, wo Handel getrieben wird und wo man sich vergnügt. Es gibt in Ägypten Tausende von Heiligen, zu denen sich regelmäßig neue gesellen. Auch gibt es Tausende von *moulids*, große, an denen über eine Million Menschen teilnehmen, und kleine, für einige hundert oder noch weniger Teilnehmer.

Die Pilgerfahrt nach Mekka, die *hagg*, ist eine Verpflichtung, der jeder Moslim, Mann und Frau, der finanziell und gesundheitlich dazu in der Lage ist, wenigstens einmal in seinem Leben nachkommen sollte. Bedingt durch den wachsenden Wohlstand und die Verbesserung der Transportmittel, nimmt die Zahl der Pilger zu: 1990, ein relativ ruhiges Jahr, sah insgesamt anderthalb Millionen Pilger, von denen 73 000 Ägypter mit der Egypt Air ab Kairo, Alexandria und Luxor nach Jeddah flogen. Für den einzelnen *hagg* oder die *hagga* sowie für Verwandte, Freunde und Nachbarn ist die Pilgerfahrt nach wie vor ein großes Ereignis. Die *haggs* sind der Stolz des ganzen Dorfes, denen nach ihrer Rückkehr von den heiligen Stätten ein begeisterter Empfang bereitet wird.

Während der Abwesenheit der Pilger werden deren Häuser mit Bildern der heiligen Stätten bemalt, die sie gerade besuchen - die Ka'ba in Mekka, das Grab des Propheten in Medina usw. -, aber auch der wirkliche oder imaginäre Weg dorthin per Flugzeug, Zug, Boot, Bus, Kamel, und was der Maler sonst noch mit der Reise assoziiert, kann dazugesteuert werden: Polizisten und Zollinspektoren, seltsame Tiere, Vögel, Blumen, Palmen oder Buraq, das Pferd, das den Propheten von Jerusalem aus in den Himmel trug. Außerdem gibt es eine Vielzahl von erbaulichen Zitaten aus dem Koran oder anderen Quellen. Besonders beliebt sind: 'Hagg ausgeführt, Sünden vergeben' und 'Der Prophet hat gesagt: "Jeder, der mein Grab besucht, hat recht auf meine Fürsprache." '

Man findet diese bemalten Häuser überall in Ägypten, aber es gibt große Unterschiede im Reichtum und in der Qualität dieser Malereien. Das Erscheinungsbild eines ganzen Dorfes wird manchmal von der Phantasie und dem Können eines einzigen Malers bestimmt. Das ist zum Beispiel der Fall in Silwa Bahari - am östlichen Nilufer zwischen Edfu und Assuan gelegen -, wo 'Id Yasin 'Ali die Häuser auf beiden Seiten der Hauptstraße verziert hat. Ähnlich verfuhr 'Ali Sayyid in Ballas (Al Mahrousa) in der Nähe von Qena. Auch in Fayoum unterscheiden sich die Dörfer durch die Bemalung ihrer Häuser.

Unglücklicherweise sind die Malereien auf den Außenwänden Sonne, Wind, Staub und Regen ausgesetzt. Auch wenn es nur selten regnet, ihr Dasein ist leider befristet. Schon nach einigen Jahren verlieren sie ihre Farben und nach ein paar weiteren verschwinden sie gänzlich. In der Zwischenzeit jedoch werden andere Häuser mit neuen Bildern verziert.

Ein Teil der Fotografien befaßt sich mit Wüsten und Oasen. Das Nil-Tal und das Delta, in dem die große Mehrheit der Ägypter lebt, sind von ausgedehnten Wüsten umgeben; flach und sandig im Norden und Westen, gebirgig entlang des Roten Meeres. Im Grunde ist das bewohnte Gebiet eine einzige große Oase. In der lybischen Wüste, westlich des Nils, gibt es einige kleinere Oasen: Bahariya, Farafra, Dakhla und Kharga. Nahe der lybischen Grenze liegt Siwa, wo eine Berber-Sprache gesprochen wird. In Siwa und Kharga findet man Pharaonentempel.

An der Westküste des Roten Meeres liegen einige Orte, an denen man Wasser gefunden hat. Sie sind die Heimat der 'Ababda und der Bisharin, nicht-arabisch sprechende Völker, die den Hadendoa und anderen, das Küstengebirge und die Küstenebenen des Sudan und Eritreas bewohnenden Völkern verwandt sind. Auch in dieser Gegend gibt es Überreste der Antike: Granit-Steinbrüche, römische Wachttürme und Siedlungen.

In der Wüste Sinai liegen die Oasen sowohl an der Küste des Mittelmeeres, des Golfs von Suez und des Golfs von Akaba als auch im Inland.

Die höheren Berge bestehen meistens aus Granit, die niedrigeren Hügel aus nubischem Sandstein. In der Oase von Farafra gibt es weiße Formationen, die an Eisberge erinnern.

Ich glaube, daß die meisten der Fotografien keiner großen Einleitung bedürfen. Es handelt sich um Bilder von Schiffen, Gräbern, Fischen, alten Autos, Inschriften und verschiedenen architektonischen Bauten.

Aber vor allem wird der Leser auf eine große Anzahl Ägypter treffen. Schließlich sind es die Menschen, die das charakteristischste und charmanteste Element ihres Landes ausmachen. Ihnen ist es zu verdanken, daß Kairo, 'die Mutter der Welt', mit ihren dreizehn, vierzehn oder fünfzehn Millionen Einwohnern, nicht nur eine der sichersten, sondern auch eine der amüsantesten Städte der Welt ist. Die Ägypter sind gastfreundlich, warmherzig und tolerant; außerdem haben sie einen unerschöpflichen Sinn für Humor. Ich hoffe, daß sie auch in ferner Zukunft so bleiben werden, wie sie sind. Wir können in mehr als einer Hinsicht viel von ihnen lernen.

Jubbega, den 23. Juni 1991

14

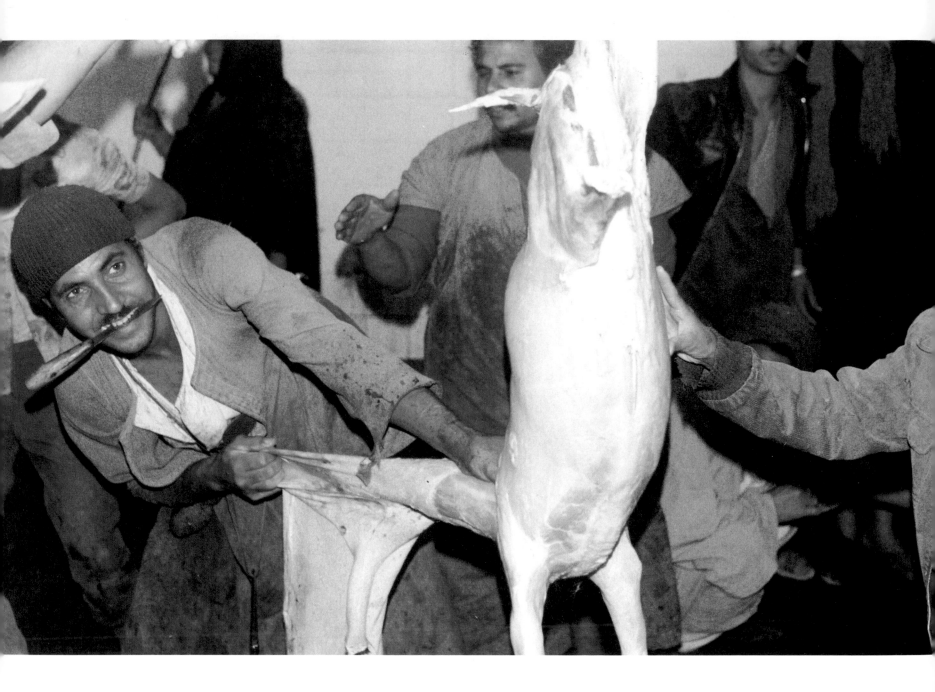

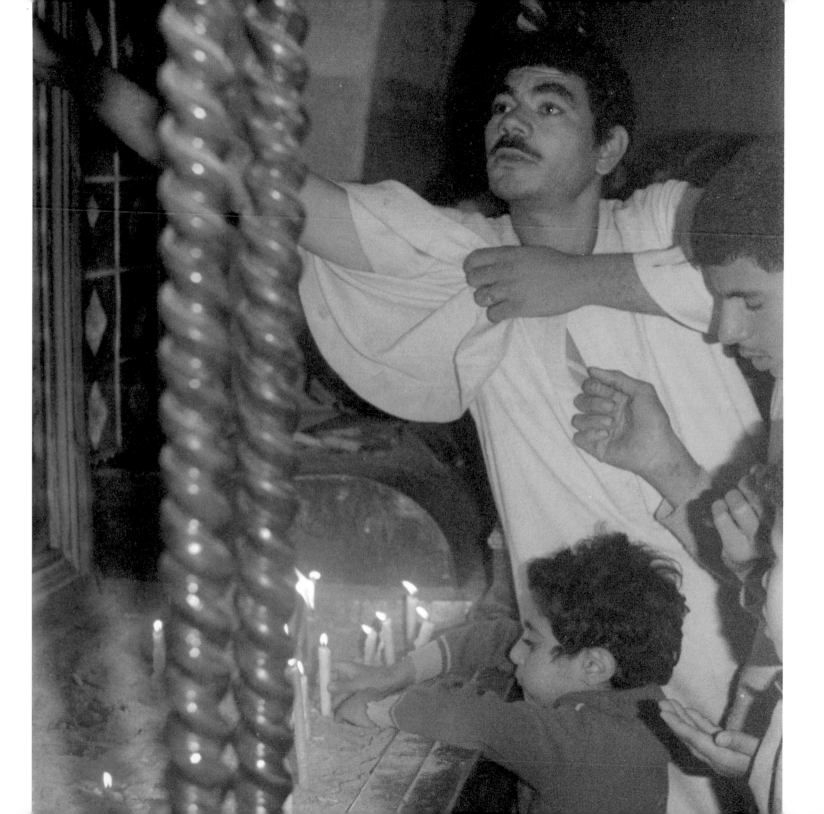

ЗА ДОЛГИЕ ГОДЫ СОВМЕСТНОГО ТРУДА
ВЫКОВАЛАСЬ И ЗАКАЛИЛАСЬ
АРАБО-СОВЕТСКАЯ ДРУЖБА,
НЕ УСТУПАЮЩАЯ ПО СВОЕЙ ПРОЧНОСТИ
САМОЙ ВЫСОТНОЙ АСУАНСКОЙ ПЛОТИНЕ
Гамаль Абдель Насер

1 A sign reading 'mines' *(algham)* warns against penetrating an uncleared area in Sinai, on the Shahira pass between Sharm al-Sheikh and Nuwayba'. Along this road there were still signs left by the Israelis with the Arabic *tamahhal* current in Palestine for 'drive slowly'. They have been replaced since by signs reading *'haddi' al-sur'a*, which means the same but is common in Egypt.

MEN

2 The owner of a coffee house sits in front of his shop in the Gamaliya, an old quarter behind the mosque of al-Husayn, with friends and neighbours. The Egyptians are renowned for their endless jokes. Perhaps they were in an even better mood than usual because al-Husayn's *moulid* was being celebrated. (Cairo)

3 An ironmonger in the Souq al-Silah. (Cairo)

4 A picture seller in al-Mu'izz li-Din Allah street smokes his first *shisha* on a cold autumn morning. (Cairo)

5 An old man is eating *koshari*, a mixture of macaroni, rice, lentils and chick peas in a red sauce. The man must be an observant Muslim, because he has a *zabiba* on his forehead. The actual meaning of *zabiba* is raisin, but here it refers to the callosity one obtains by regularly performing the Muslim prayer, during which the forehead touches the ground a number of times. (Qaransho)

6 A salesman during the *moulid* of al-Sayyida Zaynab. (Cairo)

7 A peasant, sitting on his donkey, has a Coca-Cola during the *moulid* of Abul Haggag. (Luxor)

8 A barber shaves his client in a narrow street behind the mosque of al-Sayyida Nafisa. I passed them on my way to the tombs of the 'Abbasid Caliphs which are located at the back of the mosque. (Cairo)

9 Musicians play for someone who has paid them, and who dances to their music. This *mizmar* music is mostly played in Upper Egypt, and accompanies the stick dances *(tahtib)* performed by two men in a sort of mock battle, and the horse races *(mirmah)*. These musicians were playing in a tent near the mosque of al-Husayn during his *moulid*. Spectators were allowed in on payment of a slightly higher price than usual for a glass of tea. (Cairo)

10 A man dances with a stick to the music of players from Upper Egypt during the *moulid* of al-Sayyida Zaynab. (Cairo)

11 The *rababa*-player 'Abdel Munsif Qenawi plays with his colleagues at the *moulid* of Abul Hasan al-Shazli, in the mountainous desert of Egypt's south-east corner. This *moulid* falls on *yawm 'Arafat*, 'the best day on which the sun rises', one of the days of the Mecca pilgrimage; a day of fasting and virtuous action 'if only by smiling at someone else', as a man explained at a table next to mine on a terrace at Asuan. Two days later I saw the same musicians, again playing for some stick dancers, at the *moulid* of Sheikh Idris at Kom Ombo. (Wadi Humaysara)

12 Sheikh 'Abdel Ghani 'Awdallah, accompanied by a violinist, sings songs about the Prophet and the saints for a group of Misallami dervishes at Bandara in the Delta. To this music, the dervishes dance their *zikr* to purge their souls and to draw nearer to God. (Bandara)

13 The husband of the lady in no. 43; the Pharao Amenhoteb III in the Luxor temple. Ramses II, who lived about a hundred years later, appropriated the statue by having it inscribed with a cartouche with his own name. (Luxor)

14 Men playing trictrac *(sheshbesh)* in the café al-Basfoura, built around 1950, not far from the railway station at Sohag.

15 In the *salakhana* of the monastery of St. George *(Mari Girgis)*, a voluntary butcher is slaughtering a goat. The goat has been offered to the monastery by a pilgrim, probably in redemption of a vow. The skin, the entrails and one quarter of the meat goes to the monastery; the rest is returned to the donor.
The *moulid* of St. George is one of the most important Coptic pilgrimages in Upper Egypt. The monastery is situated near Armant, on the west bank of the Nile between Luxor and Esna. (Riziq)

16 Jewish pilgrims slaughter a goat on the 103rd anniversary of the death of Yaakov Abu Khatzeira, the only Jewish saint in Egypt. The visitors are mostly from France, Morocco, where Abu Khatzeira was born, and Israel, where his nephew Baba Sali, who died not long ago, is venerated and where a younger member of the family, Aaron Abu Khatzeira, is member of parliament and a former minister. (Damanhour)

17 The camel butcher 'Abdul Ghani Ellewa has set up shop in a tomb during the *moulid* of Sidi 'Ali Zayn al-'Abidin.

The entire *moulid* takes place in the cemeteries surrounding Sidi 'Ali's mosque. (Cairo)

18 A sheep butcher in the Husayniya, the popular quarter north of Bab al-Futouh centred around the mosque which contains the tomb of Sidi 'Ali al-Bayoumi. It is said that most butchers in this area belong to the sufi order of the Bayoumiya. (Cairo)

19 A taxi driver and his mascot. (Alexandria)

20 A man with his family on a motor bike tries to make his way through a crowd after the procession for the Prophet's Birthday, *mawlid al-nabi*. Motor bikes with three, four or more passengers constitute a permanent feature of the traffic in Egypt. (Benha)

21 A fisherman belonging to the 'Ababda tribe, on the Red Sea coast between Marsa 'Alam and Berenice. The boy is wearing an amulet.

RELIGION AND BELIEFS

22 A child's hair is sacrificed to the Muslim saint Abul Haggag during his *moulid*. (Luxor)

23 A Rifa'i sheikh writes a text to be contained in an amulet, after the Friday prayer at his *saha*. (Kafr Ibrahim al-'Aydi)

24 Paper and ball-point pens are provided on the tomb of the Coptic Pope Kyrillos (or Kyrollos) VI, so that visitors can convey their requests to the saint. The tomb is in a crypt of the church in the monastery of St. Menas *(Abu Mina)* near Alexandria. Kyrillos, who was Pope of the Coptic church between 1959 and 1971, had a special relationship with the third-century St. Menas, who sometimes assisted him in curing diseases. Kyrillos rebuilt his monastery. The tomb draws many visitors on Fridays and Sundays. (Abu Mina)

25 Pilgrims and traders have built a tented camp around the monastery of St. George for the duration of the *moulid*. Processions are moving through the crowds with embroidered pieces of cloth which are offered to the monastery. (Riziq)

26, 27 A servant *(qarabni)* of the monastery of Dayr al-Shahid Mari Boktor stamps the holy bread *(qurban)* with a cross in a room near the church founded by the Byzantine empress Helena. The man was 58 years old, 45 of which he spent

working for the monastery. His wife is looking on.
In this area, on the west bank of the Nile north of Luxor, there are seven old monasteries. ('Azab)

28 A dervish of the Ahmadiya order stands at the entrance of the great mosque of Sheikh Ahmad al-Badawi. I never asked his name but I saw him regularly at various *moulids* in the Delta, where he took an active part in the *zikr*. (Tanta)

29 A Coptic pilgrim tries to touch an icon without setting fire to the sleeve of his *gallabiya*. The Copts like to have physical contact with holy objects. At the monastery of al-Amir Tadros in Cairo, and in other churches as well, there are wooden cylinders containing the relics of various saints used to cure diseases: three Sundays in a row, they are rolled over the afflicted spot. Many of the patients are Muslims. (Riziq)

30 Taxi no. 16 from Sohag is protected against the Evil Eye by two blue eyes glued to its nose. Above the eyes, the words 'God is most great' *(Allahu akbar)*. (Sohag)

31 A coach bears a somewhat unusual hand (of Fatima?) and blue eyes against the Evil Eye. (Karnak)

32 The ice-cream vendor 'Id 'Abbas takes no risks: he displays the hand of Fatima, the number 5 in two configurations referring to its fingers, a blue eye and *'Allahu akbar.'* (Cairo, *moulid* of Ahmad al-Rifa'i)

33 A swing is protected by the hand of Fatima.
On the banner is the Muslim confession of faith: 'There is no god but God, Muhammad is the messenger of God': *La ilaha illa 'llah, Muhammad rasoul Allah.* (Alexandria)

34 Near the eleventh-century city gate of Bab al-Futouh dervishes have pitched a tent for the *moulid* of Sidi 'Ali al-Bayoumi. The minaret belongs to the mosque of al-Hakim bi-Amr Allah. (Cairo)

35 Two dervishes enjoy a *zikr* of the Dayfiya order at half past nine in the morning during the *moulid* of Abul Hasan al-Shazli. (Wadi Humaysara)

WOMEN

36 A lady braves the traffic at Tal'at Harb square, formerly Suleiman Pasha square, in the centre of Cairo.

37 A peasant woman has a glass of tea during a *moulid* in the Khanka cemetery near Cairo. In this cemetery there are the shrines of six or seven saints, all less than twenty years dead.

38 Coptic women are waiting for the icon of St. George to pass in a procession. (Riziq)

39 Girls on a swing at Bulaq at the *moulid* of al-Sultan Abul 'Ela. The boss helps one of them to make a full circle. On the crossbeam, protecting them from accidents, is the hand of Fatima. (Cairo)

40 A girl sells lemonade and tamarind at the Christian *moulid* of St. Damiana in the Delta near Mansoura. (Belqas)

41 An 'Ababda girl fills a leather water bag at a shallow well. That morning, we were in search of the ruins of a Roman town in the mountainous hinterland of Berenice on the Red Sea; a stretch by Land Rover, and from there on foot with a guide. At the end of a narrow gorge we turned right, and there she sat with her father, some camels and many goats; the only living beings within miles. (Shenshef)

42 Clouds of incense hang around a saleswoman at the *moulid* of the Sayyida Zaynab. The bigger *moulids* such as this one have important economic aspects: not only incense, rosaries and Korans are sold, but also pots, pans, toys, clothes and large amounts of food and drink. (Cairo)

43 A queen, her hand touching the calf of her husband and Pharao Amenhoteb III, stands in the Luxor temple. Having been buried in sand until sixty years ago, she is very well preserved though three thousand years old. I fell in love with this little statue in 1959, and never failed to look her up whenever I was in Luxor.

44 Red sugar dolls are sold at the *moulid* of Abul Haggag in Luxor. Their shape is typical for Upper Egypt. In Cairo, sugar dolls are dressed in clothes of coloured paper for the birthday of the Prophet. (Luxor)

45 The goddess Hathor is represented on a pillar of the Ptolemaic temple of Kom Ombo.

THE MECCA PELGRIMAGE

46 The house of *al-Hāgg* Zaki Fouli 'Abdel Galil and *al-Hāgga*, his wife. On the wall, among other texts: 'Whoever visits my tomb is entitled to my intercession' and 'Hagg

performed, sins forgiven.' Painted in 1975. (Danfiq, west bank between Qurna and Ballas)

47 Pilgrims returning from Mecca are welcomed back to their village somewhere in Upper Egypt. They sit in taxis, at the rear of the joyful procession.

48 The house of *al-Hāgg* Mahmoud Farhat, decorated by a painter from the town of Fayoum. The text says: 'The Prophet has said: "Whoever visits my tomb is entitled to my intercession." ' Dated 20.9.1983. (I'lam, Fayoum)

49 The house of *al-Hāgga* Badi'a 'Abdel Wahhab, who travelled to Mecca in 1984. Next to the door are the names of the first four, righteous caliphs: Abu Bakr, 'Umar, 'Uthman and 'Ali. Over the door and windows are the *hāgga's* name and the date of her pilgrimage as well as some of God's ninety-nine 'most beautiful names': 'He is God – there is no god but He – the Merciful, the Compassionate, the King, the Most Holy, the Giver of Immunity, the Protector, the Inspirer of Trust, the Glorious, the Almighty, the Very Great, the Creator, the Maker, the Former...' (Amarna)

50 The house of *al-Hāgg* Kamal, son of *al-Hāgg* 'Abdel Sami' Isma'il, painted by 'Ali Sayyid who was then in his sixties. Kamal visited Mecca in 1986. Typical for 'Ali Sayyid's work is Buraq, the horse with the human face that carried the Prophet on his journey from Jerusalem to Heaven. We also see the Prophet's tomb mosque in Medina, a pulpit *(minbar)*, the texts mentioned in no. 46, 'Success comes only through God', 'The hagg is the most illustrious reward', *'Allahu akbar'* and, from the Koran: 'Say: "God is the Lord." ' (Ballas/Al-Mahrousa)

51 Paintings by 'Id Yasin 'Ali. At the left: 'The full moon has risen over us' (the days of the 'white nights' when the moon is full, in the middle of the Muslim month, carry extra *baraka*) with a singer of religious songs and his listeners; in the middle: 'At your service, Oh God'; and at the right: *'Hagg* performed, sins forgiven.' (Silwa Bahari)

52 Painting fading. (Shidmoh, Fayoum)

53 Painting on the house of *al-Hāgg* 'Abdel Mawgoud Mayhoub, who visited Mecca in 1982. (Itsa, Fayoum)

54 The ship on which the journey to Mecca was made. (Ma'goun, Fayoum)

55 Ship in Minya al-Hayt, Fayoum.

FISH AND SHIPS

56 These fishermen arrived in the early morning at Faraskour, having fished on the lagoons all night, to sell their catch to middlemen who took it to market at Damietta. Some tea houses were in operation along the embankment. (Faraskour)

57 Fishing boats lie on the shore of Lake Qaroun in Fayoum. This salt lake, situated in a depression below sea level, receives its water from a Nile branch, the Bahr Yousef, which irrigates the Fayoum oasis. It is stocked with fish fry from the Mediterranean. (Shakshouk)

58 Wooden ships lie on the shore of the Red Sea. I do not know if they were still in use and, if so, for what purpose. (Qusayr)

59 Sailing barges are unloading stones at Esna. During the sixties, the Nile and the navigable canals were filled with these ships. Now, they are mostly used for hauling stones or bricks on specific stretches of the river. For the rest, lorries have taken over.

60 Heads of small sharks on the beach at Dahab on the Gulf of 'Aqaba. (Dahab, Sinai)

61 Wooden ships. The location is the same as in no. 58.

62 The fish restaurant of *al-Hāgg* Hasan Mahmoud Abu Tahoun is made ready for the *moulid* of Sidi Ibrahim al-Desouqi. Inside, a quotation from the Koran: 'And We made from the water everything that lives.' (Desouq)

63 A mermaid and merman adorn the 'Nile Fish Firm' just outside Kom Ombo along the highway to Asuan.

TRANSPORT

64 A railway crossing at Kafr al-Sheikh, in the northern part of the Delta. The train is approaching. Attached to a pole in the background are signs with the names of doctors, dentists and lawyers, as is the custom in provincial towns.

65 The *'turmāy'*, i.e., the tram. This one, no. 4163, goes to Matariya.The trams are gradually being replaced by buses. (Cairo)

66 The new owner of a camel tries, in vain so far, to get it into his lorry. Camels tend to be recalcitrant animals; especially after the long journey endured before reaching the market at Embaba - more than a month's walk from Sudan; crossing the Nile by ferry at Draw; train or lorry from Draw to Cairo - they are not very much in the mood for another ride. (Embaba, Cairo)

67 Mustafa, our driver, has a cousin in a village on the east bank south of Assiut. We went to see him on our way to the deep south. The village turned out to be a staging post for taxis all dating from around 1940. This was our first contact with the phenomenon of antique taxis, which are concentrated in places endowed with garages catering to certain types of cars. Generally, the original engines have been replaced with sturdy Yugoslavian diesel engines.
These cars are mostly seen in the countryside, and sometimes provide a more or less regular service, for instance, between Baba and al-Feshn, south of Beni Sueif. There, too, we see mostly American cars from around 1940. Fords from 1946 and '47 (no. 30) are in use further south, in Sohag. Tema boasts a Studebaker of the first streamlined type. (Sahel Selim)

68 Long ago, this Chevrolet Bel-Air (Beheira taxi no. 3222) was the private car of the famous singer Farid al-Atrash. The man leaning over it is the superintendent of the taxi stand. (Ityay al-Baroud)

69 In the Village of the Blue Chevrolets in the governorate of Kafr al-Sheikh, the camera caused the customary merriment. These cars reminded me of the grey Chevrolet my father bought in 1947, when there were only a few cars in The Netherlands. I used to be very proud of it. One of the cars carries the inscription *'Allahu akbar.'*

70 A car carries *zirs*, used to keep the water cool, between Asuan and Luxor. Until recently, these pots were mostly transported on heavily loaded barges that drifted down the Nile.

71 Abu Khalid leaves Cairo with his cart towards the south. The text reads: 'I trust in God. Go in peace, Abu Khalid.' (Giza)

BUILDINGS

72 The northern city wall of medieval Cairo near Bab al-Nasr, one early morning. There are extensive cemeteries on the right-hand side.The minaret is the same one as in no. 34.

73 Houses near the station of Sohag. In the building on the right is the Hotel Sohag, and also, according to the nameplates, the lawyers Gamal Hasan, Muhammad Yousef 'Abdel Latif, 'Ala' al-Tarabishi, Ahmad Shawqi Mahmoud, Muhammad Mustafa and Mustafa Ibrahim, an engineer's bureau and an accountant.

74 The fourth-century monastery of St. George (*Mari Girgis*) al-Hadidi is situated in the Coptic village of Mari Girgis, near Akhmim. It was deserted for a long time, but has now been restored and is inhabited by three monks from the St. Samuel (*Amba Samwil*) monastery near Minya since 1987. A group of Coptic children from Sohag were visiting. A few miles from there are three more old monasteries: al-Shuhada', al-'Adhra and al-Mallak. (Mari Girgis)

75 A place of prayer (*masgid*) in the open air painted blue and red, near Nag' Hamadi. There were a number of *masgids* like this one within an area of only a few square miles.

76 This mosque is located halfway between Marsa Matrouh and the oasis of Siwa, at Bir al-Nuss (Halfway Well). In the oil drum there is water for the ritual washings.

77 Husayn Sultan's 'Super market' is situated on the Mediterranean coast west of Alexandria.

78 Haydar's shop on the beach at 'Agami near Alexandria, closed for the winter. The text reads: *'Allahu akbar.'*

INSCRIPTIONS

79 The restoration of democracy in the eighties brought a wealth of election posters, the best of which were designed by al-Wafd; a right-of-centre party which had played a major role during the first half of this century, was banned by Nasser, and had now been readmitted. 'Al-Wafd is the hope', this poster proclaims showing a lady impersonating Egypt leaning on the Parliament building.
Behind the fence a new sewerage system was being built, a gigantic enterprise which made large parts of the city even more chaotic than usual. The mirrors were sold by someone who had claimed this spot for the duration of the *moulid* of the Sayyida Zaynab. (Cairo)

80 'Vote Wafd!' urges the poster on the left, showing the party's emblem. The one on the right says: 'The Wafd is the Future', illustrated by pictures of Saad Zaghlul and Nahhas Pasha, long dead, and the leader of the moment, Sarrag al-Din,

who was then in his eighties. In the right-hand lower corner, minarets and church towers feature al-Wafd as a party for all religions. (Cairo)

81 Coptic Christians have engraved crosses and the Christ monogram ICXC on the top of Moses Mountain in Sinai, behind the monastery of St. Catherine's.

82 Disciples of the Rifa'i sheikh Fathi Hasan Abu Shousha from Minshat Bakhati in the district of Shibin al-Kom, Menoufiya, announce their presence in the tent on the right-hand side, during the *moulid* of Abul 'Abbas al-Mursi. In the corners are the names of the first caliphs. (Alexandria)

83 Near the old granite quarries in Wadi Hamamat, in the mountains along the Red Sea on the road between Qift and Qusayr, this cartouche of Ramses II is one of many inscriptions from the Pharaonic and the Greco-Roman period.

84 The Asuan High Dam was built by the USSR in the sixties. A memorial on top of the dam bears the following inscriptions in Arabic and Russian: 'Long years of united labour have erected a monument for Arab-Soviet friendship which, in value and as a symbol, is no less important than the monument of the High Dam [itself]. Gamal Abdel Nasser.'
And, in the corners:
'The High Dam is a battle which has resulted in victory, and this victory is the victory of free people... the victory of the will... the victory of well-ordered scientific exertion... the victory of the great Soviet-Arab friendship and the victory of freedom, peace and progress.
Anwar al-Sadat.' Shortly after these texts were written, the Soviets were ignominiously removed from Egypt.
Sadat's portrait and text were obviously added after the completion of the monument; somewhat like the Pharao Ramses usurping Amenhoteb's statue (no. 13). (Asuan)

85 At the *moulid* of St. Damiana in the Delta near Mansoura, the sweets seller Girgis Shawqi Butros displays his patron saint *Mari Girgis*. The sign gives a list of Christian *moulid*s where Girgis sells his sweets: St. Damiana, Mari Girgis at Kafr al-Dawar, the Holy Virgin at Mostorod near Cairo, Mari Girgis at Mit Damsis, St. Barsoum the Naked, and St. Theresa near Assiut. (Belqas)

DESERT AND OASIS

86 At Bir Murr (The Bitter Well) hangs a goat skin

containing water. The Red Sea is in the background. (Berenice)

87 Members of the 'Ababda tribe have hung their possessions out of reach of their goats in a *wadi* at the foot of mount Pentedactylus, not far from the Sudanese border on the Red Sea coast. The sun was setting, and we camped in the neighbourhood under the watchful eye of some soldiers, for this was a military area.

88 An oasis in the sea: mangrove trees off the Red Sea coast between Marsa 'Alam and Berenice.

89 Rock formations resembling icebergs north of the oasis of Farafra.

90 Rocks of granite in the First Cataract, just upstream of Asuan. In this area, the desert reaches down to the Nile.

91 Not far from the inscriptions between Qift and Qusayr (no. 83) there is an old Egyptian sarcophagus, hewn, broken and abandoned on the spot. The granite from these quarries used to be rolled to the Nile on wooden beams, a distance of almost one hundred kilometres, and carried downstream by boat.

92 In the village of al-Qasr in the oasis of Dakhla, the shape of the local pottery is reminiscent of submarines.

93 House of a *hāgg* in the oasis of Farafra.

TOMBS

94 In 1981, Sidi Nassar obtained this shrine because he had appeared in an old woman's dream. Nothing else is known about him. During the construction, forty skulls were found and entombed in the *maqam*. (Kinayyiset al-Dahriya)

95 Three of the thirty-nine holy tombs in the village of Kinayyiset al-Dahriya, in the north-western Delta.
The nearest one is that of Sidi Hamouda. Among the palm trees in the background lies Sidi Nassar, and to the right Sheikh Ahmad al-Zekayri. In the village there is also a sacred *gemayza* tree, called Sidi Khadr.
It is hoped that one more saint will appear in the village, in order to complete the magic number of 40.

96 Graves made of unbaked bricks *(toub akhdar)* near Ashmunayn, in the Minya region. Although a number of

these graves have a dome, they have no connection with saints.

97 *Déjeuner sur l'herbe* in the Khanka cemetery during one of the numerous *moulid*s celebrated there.

98 Tomb of Sheikh Zayed at Kafr al-'Arab, between Birma and Basyoun in the Delta. The tombs of saints almost invariably have a dome. A number of Muslim holy graves occupy places where a Christian saint was venerated before, and a Pharaonic deity in still earlier times. The trees are sycamores, *gemayzas*, which have been associated with holy places since antiquity.

99 In his painted tomb at Halfa Bahari, not far from Nag' Hamadi, the deceased is remembered by his rosary, water pipe, coffee or tea pot and umbrella. I have not seen graves painted in this fashion anywhere else in Egypt.

100 In the middle of Assiut, there is the tomb of Sheikh 'Ali 'Abdel Da'im 'Ali, who died in 1967. In the *zirs* there is water for the thirsty.

101 'Ababda tombs on the Red Sea coast between Marsa 'Alam and Berenice. Visitors leave a flag.

1   Un signe disant 'mines' (algham) défend de pénétrer dans une aire non nettoyée au Sinaï, sur le col Shahira entre Sharm al-Cheikh et Nuwayba'. Le long de cette route il y avait encore des signes laissés par les Israéliens avec le *tamahhal* arabe, terme courant en Palestine pour dire 'roulez lentement'. Depuis lors ils ont été remplacés par 'haddi' al-sur'a' ce qui veut dire la même chose, mais qui est le terme courant en Egypte.

HOMMES

2   Le propriétaire d'un café avec des amis et des voisins devant son commerce dans le Gamaliya, un vieux quartier derrière la mosquée d'al-Husayn. Les Egyptiens sont réputés pour leurs plaisanteries intarissables. Ils étaient peut-être d'humeur encore plus joyeuse que d'habitude à cause de la célébration du *moulid* d'al-Husayn. (Le Caire)

3   Un quincaillier au Souq al-Silah. (Le Caire)

4   Un vendeur d'illustrations dans la rue al-Mu'izz li-Din Allah fume son premier *shisha* un matin froid d'automne. (Le Caire)

5   Un vieillard mangeant du *koshari*, un mélange de macaroni, riz, lentilles et pois chiches dans une sauce rouge. L'homme doit être un musulman consciencieux, parce qu'il porte sur le front une *zabiba*. Le sens actuel de *zabiba* est raisin, mais ici *zabiba* se rapporte à la callosité qui se forme quand on accomplit régulièrement la prière musulmane pendant laquelle le front touche plusieurs fois le sol. (Qaransho)

6   Un marchand le jour du *moulid* d'al-Sayyida Zaynab. (Le Caire)

7   Un paysan assis sur son âne, boit un coca le jour du *moulid* d'Abul Haggag. (Louxor)

8   Un barbier fait la barbe à son client dans une rue étroite derrière la mosquée d'al-Sayyida Nafisa. J'y passais en allant aux tombes des califes Abbassides derrière la mosquée. (Le Caire)

9   Musiciens jouant pour quelqu'un qui leur a donné de la monnaie et qui danse aux sons de leur musique. Cette musique *mizmar* se joue le plus souvent dans la Haute-Egypte et accompagne les danses à bâton *(tahtib)* exécutées par deux hommes dans une sorte de combat simulé et les courses de chevaux *(mirmah)*. Les musiciens jouaient dans une tente près de la mosquée d'al-Husayn lors de son *moulid*. Des spectateurs étaient admis en payant un prix un peu plus élevé que d'habitude pour un verre de thé. (Le Caire)

10   Un homme danse avec un bâton aux sons de la musique faite par des musiciens de Haute-Egypte lors du *moulid* d'al-Sayyida Zaynab. (Le Caire)

11   Le joueur de *rababa*, 'Abdel Munsif Qenawi, joue avec ses collègues le jour du *moulid* d'Abul Hasan al-Shazli, dans le désert montagneux dans le sud-est de l'Egypte. Ce *moulid* tombe *yawm 'Arafat*, 'le meilleur jour où le soleil se lève', un des jours du pèlerinage à La Mecque, un jour de carême et d'action vertueuse 'si ce n'est que par une sourire adressée à quelqu'un d'autre' comme disait un homme assis à une table à côté de la mienne à une terrasse à Assuan. Deux jours après je voyais les mêmes musiciens jouer de nouveau pour quelques danseurs à bâton le jour du *moulid* du cheikh Idris à Kom Ombo. (Wadi Humaysara)

12   Le cheikh 'Abdel Ghani 'Awdallah, accompagné d'un violiniste, chante des chansons sur le Prophète et les saints pour un groupe de derviches Misallami à Bandara, dans le delta. Aux sons de cette musique les derviches dansent leur *zikr* afin d'épurer leurs âmes et de s'approcher de Dieu. (Bandara)

13   Le mari de la femme représentée à la photo 43; le pharaon Amenhoteb III, au temple de Louxor. Ramsès II, qui vécut une centaine d'années après, s'appropriait la statue en y faisant mettre un cartouche avec l'inscription de son propre nom. (Louxor)

14   Hommes jouant au trictrac *(sheshbesh)* au café al-Basfoura, construit vers 1950, pas loin de la gare de Sohag.

15   Dans la *salakhana* du monastère du saint Georges *(Mari Girgis)* un boucher volontaire abat une chèvre. La chèvre a été offerte au monastère par un pèlerin, peut-être en accomplissant d'un vœu. La peau, les entrailles et un quart de la viande sont pour le monastère; le reste retourne au donateur. Le *moulid* du saint Georges compte parmi les plus importants pèlerinages coptes dans la Haute-Egypte. Le monastère est situé près d'Armant, sur la rive ouest du Nil entre Louxor et Esna. (Riziq)

16   Des pèlerins juifs abattent une chèvre au 103e anniversaire de la mort de Yaakov Abu Khatzeira, le seul saint juif en Egypte. Les visiteurs viennent pour la plus grande partie de France, du Maroc, pays de naissance d'Abu Khatzeira, et d'Israël où est vénéré son neveu Baba Sali qui est mort il n'y a pas longtemps et où un parent plus jeune, Aaron Abu Khatzeira, est parlementaire et ancien-ministre. (Damanhour)

17   Le boucher de chameaux, 'Abdul Ghani Ellewa, a monté un commerce dans une tombe pendant le *moulid* de Sidi 'Ali Zayn al-'Abidin. Tout le *moulid* a lieu aux cimetières autour de la mosquée de Sidi 'Ali. (Le Caire)

18   Un boucher de moutons dans le Husayniya, le quartier populaire au nord de Bab al-Futouh au centre duquel se trouve la mosquée abritant la tombe de Sidi 'Ali al-Bayoumi. On dit que la plupart des bouchers dans cette région appartiennent à l'ordre soufi d'al-Bayoumiya. (Le Caire)

19   Un chauffeur de taxi et sa mascotte. (Alexandrie)

20   Un homme avec sa famille en motocyclette essaie de se frayer un chemin à travers la foule après la procession à l'occasion de l'anniversaire du Prophète, *mawlid al-nabi*. Des motocyclettes avec trois, quatre ou plus de passagers encore constituent un caractéristique permanent de la circulation en Egypte. (Benha)

21   Un pêcheur appartenant à la tribu 'Ababda sur la côte de la mer Rouge entre Marsa 'Alam et Bérénice. Le petit garçon porte une amulette.

RELIGION ET CROYANCE

22   Des cheveux d'un enfant sont sacrifiés au saint musulman Abul Haggag lors de son *moulid*. (Louxor)

23   Un cheikh Rifa'i écrit une amulette après la prière de vendredi à sa *saha*. (Kafr Ibrahim al-'Aydi)

24   On procure du papier et des stylos à bille sur la tombe du pape copte Kyrillos (ou Kyrollos) VI, de sorte que les visiteurs puissent communiquer leurs demandes au saint. La tombe se trouve dans une crypte de l'église dans le monastère du saint Menas *(Abu Mina)* près d'Alexandrie. Kyrillos, pape de l'église copte de 1959 à 1971, avait une relation particulière avec le saint Menas du troisième siècle qui l'aidait parfois dans la guérison de maladies. Kyrillos a reconstruit son monastère. La tombe attire de nombreux visiteurs les vendredis et dimanches. (Abu Mina)

25 Pèlerins et marchands ont monté un douar autour du monastère du saint Georges pour la durée du *moulid*. Des processions passent à travers la foule avec des châles brodés qui seront offerts au monastère. (Riziq)

26, 27 Un serviteur (*qarabni*) du monastère de Dayr al-Shahid Mari Boktor tasse le pain saint (*qurban*) avec une croix dans une pièce près de l'église fondée par l'impératrice byzantine Hélène. L'homme avait 58 ans dont 45 passés au service du monastère. Sa femme regarde. Dans cette zone, sur la rive ouest du Nil au nord de Louxor, il y a sept vieux monastères. ('Azab)

28 Un derviche de l'ordre d'Ahmadiya à l'entrée de la grande mosquée du cheikh Ahmad al-Badawi. Je ne lui ai jamais demandé son nom, mais je l'ai vu régulièrement à différents *moulid* dans le delta, où il prenait une part active au *zikr*. (Tanta)

29 Un pèlerin copte essaie de toucher une icône sans que la manche de sa *gallabiya* ne prenne feu. Les coptes aiment le contact physique avec les objets saints. Dans le monastère d'al-Amir Tadros au Caire, de même que dans d'autres églises, on trouve des rouleaux en bois qui contiennent les reliques de différents saints qu'on utilise pour guérir des maladies: pendant trois dimanches successifs on les roule sur l'endroit affecté. Parmi les malades il y a beaucoup de musulmans. (Riziq)

30 Le taxi numéro 16 de Sohag est protégé contre le Mauvais Œil par deux yeux bleus, collés sur son nez. Au-dessus des yeux les mots 'Dieu est infiniment grand' (*Allahu akbar*). (Sohag)

31 Une carrosse porte une main un peu inhabituelle (de Fatima?) et des yeux bleus contre le Mauvais Œil. (Karnak)

32 Le vendeur de glaces 'Id 'Abbas ne prend aucun risque: il montre la main de Fatima, deux fois le numéro 5 qui se réfère à ses doigts, un œil bleu et '*Allahu akbar*.' (Le Caire, *moulid* d'Ahmad al-Rifa'i)

33 Une balançoire est protégée par la main de Fatima. Sur la bannière est inscrite la confession musulmane de foi: 'Il n'y a pas de divinité si ce n'est Allah et Mahomet est l'envoyé d'Allah': *La ilaha illa 'llah, Muhammad rasoul Allah*. (Alexandrie)

34 Près de la porte de ville du onzième siècle de Bab al-Futouh des derviches ont monté une tente pour le *moulid* de Sidi 'Ali al-Bayoumi. Le minaret appartient à la mosquée d'al-Hakim bi-Amr Allah. (Le Caire)

35 Deux derviches se complaisaient à regarder un *zikr* de l'ordre de Dayfiya à neuf heures et demie du matin lors du *moulid* d'Abul Hasan al-Shazli. (Wadi Humaysara)

FEMMES

36 Une femme affronte la circulation sur la place Tal'at Harb, auparavant la place Suleiman Pasha au centre du Caire.

37 Une femme de la campagne boit un verre de thé lors du *moulid* au cimetière de Khanka près du Caire. Cette cimetière contient les reliquaires de six ou sept saints, tous morts il y a moins de vingt ans.

38 Femmes coptes attendant l'icône du saint Georges qui passera en procession. (Riziq)

39 Filles sur une balançoire à Bulaq, le jour du *moulid* d'al-Sultan Abul 'Ela. Le patron aide une des filles à faire tout le cercle. Sur le racinal il y a la main de Fatima qui doit les protéger contre les accidents. (Le Caire)

40 Une jeune fille vend de la limonade et du tamarin lors du *moulid* chrétien de la sainte Damiana, dans le delta près de Mansoura. (Belqas)

41 Une fille de la tribu 'Ababda remplit une outre en cuir de l'eau d'un puits peu profond. Ce matin nous étions à la recherche des ruines d'une ville romaine dans l'arrière-pays montagneux de Bérénice sur la mer Rouge; en partie en Land Rover et ensuite à pied avec un guide. A la fin d'une gorge étroite nous prenions à droite et la voilà assise avec son père, quelques chameaux et un grand nombre de chèvres, les seuls êtres vivants dans un rayon de plusieurs kilomètres. (Shenshef)

42 Des nuages d'encens autour d'une vendeuse lors du *moulid* d'al Sayyida Zaynab. Les *moulid* d'une plus grande importance comme celui-ci ont de notables aspects économiques: on ne vend pas seulement de l'encens, des rosaires et des corans, mais des pots, casseroles, jouets, vêtements et de grandes quantités de nourriture et de boisson. (Le Caire)

43 Une reine dans le temple de Louxor avec sa main sur le mollet de son mari, le pharaon Amenhoteb III. Comme elle a été ensevelie dans le sable jusqu'à il y a soixante ans, elle est très bien conservée malgré ses trois mille ans. Je tombais amoureux de cette petite statue en 1959 et je ne manquais jamais de lui rendre visite quand j'étais à Louxor.

44 Des poupées de sucre rouge sont vendues au *moulid* d'Abul Haggag à Louxor. Leur forme est caractéristique pour la Haute-Egypte. Au Caire, les poupées de sucre sont habillées de papier coloré pour l'anniversaire du Prophète. (Louxor)

45 La déesse Hathor représentée sur le pilier du temple ptolémaïque de Kom Ombo.

LE PÈLERINAGE À LA MECQUE

46 La maison d'*al-Hagg* Zaki Fouli 'Abdel Galil et d'*al-Hagga*, sa femme. Sur le mur: 'Tous ceux qui visitent ma tombe peuvent revendiquer mon intercession' et '*Hagg* accompli, péchés pardonnés.' Peint en 1975. (Danfiq, rive ouest entre Qurna et Ballas)

47 Des pèlerins retournant de La Mecque sont accueillis dans leur village quelque part dans la Haute-Egypte. Ils se trouvent dans des taxis qui suivent la procession joyeuse.

48 La maison d'*al-Hagg* Mahmoud Farhat, décorée par un peintre de la ville d'al-Fayoum. Le texte veut dire: 'Le Prophète a dit: "Tous ceux qui visitent ma tombe, peuvent revendiquer mon intercession"', en date du 20.9.1983. (I'lam, le Fayoum)

49 La maison d'*al-Hagga* Badi'a 'Abdel Wahhab, qui voyageait à La Mecque en 1984. A côté de la porte figurent les noms des quatre premiers califes: Abu Bakr, 'Umar, 'Uthman et 'Ali. Au-dessus de la porte et de la fenêtre le nom de la *hagga* et la date de son pèlerinage et quelques-uns des quatre-vingt-dix-neuf 'plus beaux' noms de Dieu: 'Il est Dieu, il n'y a pas de divinité si ce n'est Lui - le Miséricordieux, le Charitable, le Roi, le Saint des saints, le Donateur d'Immunité, le Protecteur, l'Inspirateur de confiance, le Glorieux, le Tout-Puissant, le Très Grand, le Créateur, l'Auteur, le Formateur...' (Amarna)

50 La maison d'*al-Hagg* Kamal, fils d'*al-Hagg* 'Abdel Sami' Isma'il, peinte par 'Ali Sayyid qui avait alors plus de soixante ans. Kamal a visité La Mecque en 1986. Caractéristique de l'œuvre d'*'Ali Sayyid est Buraq, le cheval au visage humain qui portait le Prophète lors de son voyage de Jérusalem aux Cieux. Nous trouvons également la mosquée qui abrite la tombe du Prophète à Médine, une

chaire (minbar), les textes mentionnés au no. 46, 'Le succès n'arrive que par Dieu', 'Le hagg est la récompense la plus illustre', 'Allahu akbar' et pris dans le Coran: 'Dis: "Dieu est le Seigneur."' (Ballas/Al-Mahrousa)

51   Peintures d'Id Yasin 'Ali. A gauche: 'La pleine lune s'est levée au-dessus de nous' (les jours des 'nuits blanches', quand la lune est dans son plein, au milieu du mois musulman, portent une quantité extra de baraka) avec un chanteur de chansons religieuses et son auditoire; au milieu: 'A votre service, oh mon Dieu'; et à droite: 'Hagg accompli, péchés pardonnés.' (Silwa Bahari)

52   Peintures en voie de disparition. (Shidmoh, le Fayoum)

53   Peintures sur la maison d'al-Hāgg 'Abdel Mawgoud Mayhoub, qui visitait La Mecque en 1982. (Itsa, le Fayoum)

54   Le bateau avec lequel on a fait le voyage à La Mecque. (Ma'goun, le Fayoum)

55   Bateau à Minya al-Hayt, le Fayoum.

PÊCHEURS ET POISSONS

56   Après avoir pêché toute la nuit sur les lagunes, ces pêcheurs arrivaient au point du jour à Faraskour pour vendre leur butin à des intermédiaires qui le portaient ensuite au marché à Damiette. Quelques maisons de thé le long du quai étaient ouvertes. (Faraskour)

57   Bateaux de pêche au bord du Lac Qaroun dans le Fayoum. Ce lac salé situé dans une dépression au-dessous du niveau marin reçoit ses eaux d'une branche du Nil, le Bahr Youssef, qui irrigue l'oasis du Fayoum. Le lac est aleviné à partir de la Méditerranée. (Shakshouk)

58   Bateaux en bois sur la côte de la mer Rouge. Je ne sais pas s'ils sont toujours utilisés et si oui, dans quel but. (Qusayr)

59   Bateaux à voile dont on débarque des pierres, à Esna. Pendant les années soixante le Nil et les canaux navigables étaient pleins de ces bateaux. Actuellement ils servent le plus souvent à transporter des pierres ou briques sur certains trajets du fleuve. Le reste de leur tâche a été pris par des camions.

60   Têtes de petits requins sur la plage à Dahab sur le Golfe d''Aqaba. (Dahab, Sinai)

61   Des bateaux en bois. L'endroit est le même que celui du no. 58.

62   Le restaurant d'al-Hāgg Hasan Mahmoud Abu Tahoun est préparé au moulid de Sidi Ibrahim al-Desouqi. A l'intérieur une citation du Coran: 'Et Nous créions à partir d'eau tout ce qui vit.' (Desouq)

63   Sirène et triton parant la 'Firme Poissons du Nil' juste en dehors de Kom Ombo le long de la route nationale vers Assuan.

TRANSPORT

64   Un passage à niveau à Kafr al-Cheikh, dans la partie nord du delta. Le train arrive. Attachés à un poteau des enseignes portent les noms de médecins, dentistes et avocats, comme il est d'usage dans les villes de province. (Kafr al-Cheikh)

65   Le 'turmāy', c'est-à-dire le tramway. Celui-ci, le numéro 4163, va à Matariya. Peu à peu les tramways sont remplacés par des autocars. (Le Caire)

66   Le nouveau propriétaire d'un chameau essaie, en vain jusqu'ici, de le faire entrer dans son camion. Les chameaux ont tendance à se montrer récalcitrants et surtout après avoir supporté le long voyage avant d'arriver au marché d'Embaba - une marche de plus d'un mois à partir du Soudan; traversée du Nil en ferry-boat à Draw; de Draw au Caire par le train ou en camion - ils ne sont pas très disposés à faire un autre voyage. (Embaba, Le Caire)

67   Mustafa, notre chauffeur, avait un cousin dans un village sur la rive est au sud d'Assiout. Nous allions le voir sur notre route vers le sud lointain. Le village s'avérait être un arrêt fixe pour des taxis qui dataient tous d'environ 1940. C'était notre premier contact avec le phénomène de taxis d'époque, concentrés dans des lieux dotés de garages spécialisés dans certains types de voitures. En général un diesel solide yougoslave a remplacé le moteur original.
Ces voitures se rencontrent le plus souvent à la campagne et entretiennent parfois un service plus ou moins régulier, par exemple entre Baba et al-Feshn, au sud de Beni Sueif. Là aussi nous rencontrions le plus souvent des voitures américaines d'environ 1940. Plus vers le sud, à Sohag, les Ford de 1946 et 1947 (no. 30) sont en usage. Tema est l'heureux propriétaire d'une Studebaker du premier type caréné. (Sahel Selim)

68   Dans le temps cette Chevrolet Bel-Air (taxi Beheira

numéro 3222) était la voiture privée du chanteur célèbre Farid al-Atrash. L'homme qui s'y appuie est le surveillant de la station de taxis. (Ityāy al-Baroud)

69   Au Village des Chevrolets Bleues dans le gouvernorat de Kafr al-Cheikh, le caméra causait la gaieté usuelle. Ces voitures me rappelaient la Chevrolet grise achetée par mon père en 1947 dans un temps où il n'y avait que peu de voitures aux Pays-Bas. J'en étais très fier.
Une des voitures porte l'inscription 'Allahu akbar.'

70   Une voiture chargée de zir, utilisés pour garder l'eau fraîche entre Assuan et Louxor. Il n'y a pas encore longtemps ces jarres étaient transportées surtout sur des barges lourdement chargées qui descendaient le Nil.

71   Abu Khalid quitte Le Caire avec sa charrette pour aller au sud. Le texte dit: 'Je me fie à Dieu. Pars en paix, Abu Khalid.' (Giza)

BÂTIMENTS

72   Le mur nord de la ville du Caire médiéval près de Bab al-Nasr, au petit matin. Du côté droit il y a des cimetières étendus. Le minaret est le même que celui du no. 34. (Le Caire)

73   Maisons près de la gare de Sohag. Le bâtiment à droite abrite l'hôtel Sohag et aussi, à en croire les plaques, les avocats Gamal Hasan, Muhammad Yousef 'Abdel Latif, 'Ala' al-Tarabishi, Ahmad Shawqi Mahmoud, Muhammad Mustafa et Mustafa Ibrahim, un bureau d'ingénieur et un expert-comptable.

74   Le monastère du quatrième siècle du saint Georges (Mari Girgis) al-Hadidi est situé au village copte de Mari Girgis, près d'Akhmim. Il a longtemps été abandonné, mais depuis 1987 il a été restauré et habité par trois moines du monastère du saint Samuel (Amba Samwil) près de Minya. Un groupe d'enfants coptes de Sohag le visitaient. Quelques kilomètres plus loin il y a trois autres vieux monastères: al-Shuhada', al-'Adhra et al-Mallak. (Mari Girgis)

75   Un lieu de prière (masgid) en plein air peint en bleu et en rouge, près de Nag' Hamadi. Il y avait une quantité de masgid comme celui-ci sur une surface de quelques kilomètres carrés seulement.

76   Cette mosquée est située à mi-chemin entre Marsa

Matrouh et l'oasis de Siouah, à Bir al-Nuss (Puits à mi-chemin). Le baril contient de l'eau pour l'ablution rituelle.

77 Le 'supermarché' de Husayn Sultan sur la côte méditerranéenne à l'ouest d'Alexandrie.

78 La boutique de Haydar sur la plage à 'Agami près d'Alexandrie, fermée pour l'hiver. Le texte dit: '*Allahu akbar.*'

INSCRIPTIONS

79 La restauration de la démocratie dans les années quatre-vingt a provoqué une profusion d'affiches électorales, dont les meilleures étaient dessinées par al-Wafd, un parti de droite qui avait joué un rôle important dans la première moitié de ce siècle, avait été interdit par Nasser, mais qui était maintenant de nouveau admis. 'Al-Wafd est l'espoir', proclame cette affiche sur laquelle figure une femme personnifiant l'Egypte et qui s'appuie sur la salle du Congrès.
Derrière la clôture on était en train de construire un nouveau réseau d'égouts, une entreprise énorme qui rendait de grandes parties de la ville encore plus chaotiques que d'habitude. Les glaces étaient vendues par quelqu'un qui avait réclamé cet endroit pour la durée du *moulid* d'al Sayyida Zaynab. (Le Caire)

80 'Votez Wafd!' crie l'affiche à gauche avec l'emblème du parti. L'affiche à droite dit: 'Le Wafd est l'avenir.' Elle montre les portraits de Saad Zaghlul et Nahhas Pasha, morts depuis longtemps, et du chef actuel, Sarrag al-Din, qui était alors octogénaire. Dans le coin en bas à droite des minarets et des tours d'église caractérisent al-Wafd comme un parti pour toutes les religions. (Le Caire)

81 Des chrétiens coptes ont gravé des croix et le monogramme du Christ ICXC au sommet de la montagne de Moïse au Sinaï derrière le monastère de la sainte Catherine.

82 Des disciples du cheikh Rifa'i, Fathi Hasan Abu Shousha de Minshat Bakhati dans le district de Shibin al-Kom, Menoufiya, annoncent leur présence dans la tente à droite lors du *moulid* d'Abul 'Abbas al-Mursi. Dans les coins les noms des premiers califes. (Alexandrie)

83 Près des vieilles fosses de granit à Wadi Hamamat, dans la montagne le long de la mer Rouge sur la route entre Qift et Qusayr, ce cartouche de Ramsès II représente une des nombreuses inscriptions de la période pharaonique et greco-romaine.

84 Le haut Barrage d'Assuan a été construit par l'U.R.S.S. dans les années soixante. Un monument commémoratif porte les inscriptions suivantes en arabe et en russe:
'De longues années d'efforts concurrents ont érigé un monument de l'amitié arabe-soviétique qui, quant à la valeur et comme symbole, n'est pas moins important que le monument du haut Barrage [lui-même]. Gamal Abdel Nasser.' Et, dans les coins: 'Le haut Barrage est une bataille qui a abouti à la victoire et cette victoire est la victoire du peuple libre... la victoire de la volonté... la victoire d'efforts scientifiques bien ordonnés... la victoire de la grande amitié arabe-soviétique et la victoire de la liberté, de la paix et du progrès. Anwar al-Sadate.' Peu après que ces textes furent écrits les Soviétiques furent expulsés ignominieusement de l'Egypte.
Le portrait et le texte de Sadate ont visiblement été ajoutés après l'achèvement du monument; à peu près de la même façon dont le pharaon Ramsès usurpait la statue d'Amenhoteb (no. 13). (Assuan)

85 Au *moulid* de la sainte Damiana dans le delta près de Mansourah, le vendeur de sucreries Girgis Shawqi Butros montre son patron, le saint *Mari Girgis*. L'écriteau donne la liste des *moulid* chrétiens où Girgis vend ses sucreries: sainte Damiana, Mari Girgis à Kafr al-Dawar, la Sainte Vierge à Mostorod près du Caire, Mari Girgis à Mit Damsis, saint Barsoum le Nu, et sainte Thérèse près d'Assiout. (Belqas)

86 A Bir Murr (Le Puits Amer) une peau de chèvre contenant de l'eau est suspendue. La mer Rouge à l'arrière-plan. (Bérénice)

87 Des membres de la tribu 'Ababda ont suspendu leurs possessions hors de l'atteinte de leurs chèvres dans un oued au pied de la montagne Pentedactylus, pas loin de la frontière soudanaise sur la côte de la mer Rouge. Le soleil se couchait et nous allions camper dans les environs surveillés par quelques soldats parce que c'était une zone militaire.

88 Une oasis dans la mer: palétuviers près de la côte de la mer Rouge entre Marsa 'Alam et Bérénice.

89 Groupes de rochers ayant l'aspect d'icebergs au nord de l'oasis de Farafra.

90 Rochers granitiques dans la Première Cataracte, juste en amont d'Assuan. Dans cette région le désert s'étend jusqu'au Nil.

91 Non loin des inscriptions entre Qift et Qusayr (no. 83) se trouve un vieux sarcophage égyptien, taillé, cassé et abandonné sur place. Autrefois on roulait le granit de ces fosses sur des poutres en bois vers le Nil, une distance de près de cent kilomètres; puis il était transporté en aval en bateau.

92 Au village d'al-Qasr dans l'oasis de Dakhla, la forme des poteries locales rappelle des sous-marins.

93 Maison d'un *hāgg* dans l'oasis de Farafra.

TOMBEAUX

94 En 1981, Sidi Nassar recevait ce reliquaire pour avoir paru en rêve à une vieille femme. Personne ne sait rien d'autre à son sujet. Lors de la construction, on a trouvé quarante crânes qu'on a enseveli dans le *maqam*. (Kinayyiset al-Dahriya)

95 Trois des trente-neuf tombes saintes au village de Kinayyiset al-Dahriya sur le delta nord-ouest. La tombe la plus proche est celle de Sidi Hamouda. Parmi les palmiers à l'arrière-plan repose Sidi Nassar et à droite le cheikh Ahmad al-Zekayri. Le village possède aussi une *gemayza* sacrée, qui s'appelle Sidi Khadr. On espère que le village aura encore un autre saint afin de compléter le nombre magique de 40.

96 Tombes faites de briques crues *(toub akhdar)* près d'Ashmunayn, dans la région de Minya. Bien que quelques-unes de ces tombes portent un dôme, elles n'ont aucun rapport avec des saints.

97 'Déjeuner sur l'herbe' au cimetière de Khanka pendant un des nombreux *moulid* qui sont célébrés ici.

98 Tombe du cheikh Zayed à Kafr al-'Arab, entre Birma et Basyoun dans le delta. Les tombes des saints sont presque invariablement surmontées d'un dôme. Un nombre de tombes saintes musulmanes occupent des endroits où on vénérait avant un saint chrétien et aux temps encore plus reculés un dieu pharaonique. Les arbres sont des sycamores, *gemayza*, qui depuis l'antiquité ont été associés à des lieux saints.

99 Dans sa tombe peinte à Halfa Bahari, à faible distance de Nag' Hamadi, le décédé est commémoré par son rosaire, son narguilé, son pot à café ou à thé et son parapluie. Nulle part ailleurs en Egypte j'ai vu des tombes peintes de cette façon-ci.

100 Au centre d'Assiout se trouve la tombe du cheikh 'Ali

'Abdel Da'im 'Ali, mort en 1967. Les *zir* contiennent de l'eau pour l'assoiffé.

101 Une tombe 'Ababda sur la côte de la mer Rouge entre Marsa 'Alam et Bérénice. Les visiteurs laissent un drapeau.

Women carrying water pots wait for the train to pass. One of them wears ankle rings (*khul-khal*).
Des femmes portant des cruches à eau attendent que le train soit passé. Une d'elles porte des bracelets de cheville (*khul-khal*).
Frauen tragen Wasserkrüge und warten darauf, daß der Zug vorbeifährt. Eine von ihnen trägt Knöchel-Ringe (*khul-khal*).
(Asuan-Luxor, 1959)

1 Auf einem Schild steht 'Minen' (algham). Es warnt davor, ein ungeräumtes Gebiet in Sinai, auf dem Shahira-Paß zwischen Sharm al-Sheikh und Nuwayba', zu betreten. Auf dieser Straße gab es noch immer Schilder, die die Israelis mit tamahhal beschriftet hatten, dem arabischen Ausdruck, üblich in Palästina, für 'Langsam fahren'. Sie wurden seither gegen Schilder ausgetauscht, auf denen 'haddi' al-sur'a' steht, was das gleiche bedeutet, aber dann auf 'ägyptisch'.

MÄNNER

2 Der Besitzer eines Kaffeehauses sitzt mit Freunden und Nachbarn vor seinem Laden in der Gamalia, einem alten Viertel hinter der al-Husayn Moschee. Die Ägypter sind bekannt für ihre Witze, die kein Ende nehmen wollen. Vielleicht waren diese noch besser gelaunt als gewöhnlich, da die moulid von al-Husayn gefeiert wurde. (Kairo)

3 Ein Eisenwarenhändler im Suk al-Silah. (Kairo)

4 Ein Bilderverkäufer in der al-Mu'izz li-Din Allah Straße raucht seine erste shisha an einem kalten Morgen im Herbst. (Kairo)

5 Ein alter Mann ißt koshari, ein Gericht aus Makkaroni, Reis, Linsen und Kichererbsen in einer roten Soße. Der Mann muß ein praktizierender Moslim sein, da er auf seiner Stirn eine zabiba hat. Zabiba bedeutet eigentlich Rosine, hier aber ist die Schwiele gemeint, die sich durch regelmäßiges Ausüben des moslemischen Gebets, bei dem die Stirn mehrere Male den Boden berührt, bildet. (Qaransho)

6 Ein Verkäufer während der moulid von al-Sayyida Zaynab. (Kairo)

7 Ein Bauer, auf seinem Esel sitzend, trinkt eine Cola während der moulid von Abul Haggag. (Luxor)

7 Ein Barbier rasiert einen Kunden in einer engen Straße hinter der al-Sayyida Nafisa Moschee. Ich traf auf die zwei auf meinem Weg zu den Gräbern der 'Abbasidischen Kalifen, die hinter der Moschee liegen. (Kairo)

9 Musiker spielen für ihren Auftraggeber, der zu ihrer Musik tanzt. Diese mizmar-Musik wird meistens in Oberägypten gespielt, als Begleitung des Tanzes mit den Stöcken (tahtib), einer Art Schein-Kampfes zweier Männer, oder der Pferderennen (mirmah). Diese Musiker spielten während der moulid in einem Zelt in der Nähe der al-Husayn Moschee. Zuschauer waren unter der Bedingung zugelassen, daß sie einen etwas höheren Preis als gewöhnlich für ihr Glas Tee bezahlten. (Kairo)

10 Ein Mann tanzt mit einem Stock zur Musik der oberägyptischen Musikanten während der moulid von al-Sayyida Zaynab. (Kairo)

11 Der rababa-Spieler 'Abdel Munsif Qenawi spielt mit seinen Kollegen zur moulid von Abul Hasan al-Shazli in der gebirgigen Wüste von Ägyptens süd-östlichem Zipfel. Diese moulid fällt auf den yawm 'Arafat, den 'besten Tag, an dem die Sonne aufgeht', einer der Tage der Pilgerfahrt nach Mekka; ein Tag des Fastens und der guten Taten. 'Und sei es auch nur, indem man einem anderen zulächelt', wie ein Mann sagte, der an meinem Nebentisch auf einer Terrasse in Assuan saß. Zwei Tage später sah ich die gleichen Musiker, wiederum für Stock-Tänzer spielend, bei der moulid von Scheich Idris in Kom Ombo. (Wadi Humsayara)

12 Scheich 'Abdel Ghani 'Awdallah, begleitet von einem Violisten, singt Lieder über den Propheten und die Heiligen für eine Gruppe von Misallami-Derwischen in Bandara, im Delta. Die Derwische tanzen zu dieser Musik den zikr, um ihre Seelen zu reinigen und näher zu Gott zu gelangen. (Bandara)

13 Der Ehemann der Dame von Nr. 43, der Pharao Amenhoteb III., im Tempel von Luxor. Ramses II., der ein Jahrhundert später lebte, eignete sich die Statue an, indem er eine Kartusche mit seinem eigenen Namen einmeißeln ließ. (Luxor)

14 Männer spielen trictrac (shesbesh) im Café al-Basfoura, erbaut um 1959, nicht weit entfernt vom Bahnhof in Sohag.

15 In der salakhana des Klosters St. Georg (Mari Girgis) schlachtet ein freiwilliger Metzger eine Ziege. Die Ziege bekam das Kloster von einem Pilger geschenkt, wahrscheinlich als Einlösung eines Gelübdes. Die Haut, die Innereien und ein Viertel des Fleisches behält das Kloster; der Rest geht zurück an den Spender. Die moulid von St. Georg ist eine der wichtigsten koptischen Pilgerfahrten in Oberägypten. Das Kloster liegt in der Nähe von Armant, am Westufer des Nils zwischen Luxor und Esna. (Riziq)

16 Jüdische Pilger schlachten eine Ziege am 103. Todestage von Yaakov Abu Khatzeira, dem einzigen jüdischen Heiligen in Ägypten. Die Besucher kommen hauptsächlich aus Frankreich, Marokko, wo Abu Khatzeira geboren wurde, und Israel, wo sein Neffe Baba Sali, der vor nicht allzu langer Zeit starb, verehrt wird. Ein jüngeres Mitglied der Familie, Aaron Abu Khatzeira, war dort früher Minister und ist heute Parlamentsmitglied. (Damanhour)

17 Der Kamel-Metzger 'Abdul Ghani Ellewa hat während der moulid von Sidi 'Ali Zayn al-'Abidin einen Laden in einem Grabmal aufgemacht. Die ganze moulid findet auf den Friedhöfen bei der Sidi 'Ali Moschee statt. (Kairo)

18 Ein Schaf-Metzger in der Husayniya, dem volkstümlichen Wohnviertel nördlich von Bab al-Futouh, das die Moschee umgibt. Sie beherbergt das Grab von Sidi 'Ali. Man sagt, daß die meisten der Metzger in diesem Viertel dem Sufi-Orden der Bayoumiya angehören. (Kairo)

19 Ein Taxifahrer und sein Maskottchen. (Alexandria)

20 Ein Mann mit seiner Familie auf einem Motorrad versucht, sich nach der Prozession zu Ehren des Geburtstags des Propheten, mawlid al-nabi, einen Weg durch die Menge zu bahnen. Motorräder mit drei, vier oder mehr Passagieren sind keine Seltenheit im ägyptischen Verkehr. (Benha)

21 Ein Fischer, der zum 'Abadba Stamm gehört, an der Küste des Roten Meeres zwischen Marsa 'Alam und Berenice. Der Junge trägt ein Amulett.

RELIGION UND GLAUBENSFORMEN

22 Das Haar eines Kindes wird dem moslemischen Heiligen Abul Haggag während seiner moulid geopfert. (Luxor)

23 Ein Rifa'i Scheich beschreibt ein Amulett nach dem Freitagsgebet in seiner saha. (Kafr Ibrahim al-'Aydi)

24 Papier und Kugelschreiber werden am Grab des koptischen Popen Kyrillos (oder Kyrollos) VI. verteilt, so daß die Gläubigen dem Heiligen ihre Wünsche übermitteln können. Das Grab befindet sich in einer Krypta der Kirche des St. Menas (Abu Mina) Klosters in der Nähe von Alexandria. Kyrillos, der das Oberhaupt der koptischen Kirche von 1959 bis 1971 war, hatte eine besondere Beziehung zu dem Heiligen St. Menas aus dem 3. Jahrhundert. Dieser half ihm manchmal, Krankheiten zu kurieren, und Kyrillos baute ihm sein Kloster wieder auf. Freitags und samstags ist das Grabmal vielbesucht. (Abu Mina)

25 Pilger und Handelsleute haben für die Dauer der *moulid* ein überdachtes Lager um das Kloster von St. Georg herum gebaut. Durch die Menge bewegen sich Prozessionen mit reich verzierten Stoffstücken, die dann dem Kloster geschenkt werden. (Riziq)

26, 27 Ein Diener *(qarabni)* des Klosters von Dayr al-Shahid Mari Boktor stempelt das heilige Brot *(qurban)* mit einem Kreuz, in einem Zimmer in der Nähe der Kirche, die von der byzantinischen Kaiserin Helena gegründet wurde. Der 58 jährige Mann arbeitet seit 45 Jahren für das Kloster. Seine Frau schaut ihm zu. Es gibt in dieser Gegend, am Westufer des Nils nördlich von Luxor, sieben alte Klöster. ('Azab)

28 Ein Derwisch des Ahmadiya Ordens steht am Eingang der großen Moschee von Scheich Ahmad al-Badawi. Ich habe ihn nie nach seinem Namen gefragt, aber ich sah ihn regelmäßig bei verschiedenen *moulid*s im Delta, wo er aktiv am *zikr* teilnahm. (Tanta)

29 Ein koptischer Pilger versucht, eine Ikone zu berühren, ohne den Ärmel seiner *gallabiya* in Brand zu stecken. Die Kopten haben gerne körperlichen Kontakt mit heiligen Dingen. Im Kloster von al-Amir Tadros in Kairo sowie in anderen Kirchen gibt es Holzzylinder, die die Reliquien verschiedener Heiligen enthalten. Diese benutzt man zur Heilung von Krankheiten: An drei aufeinanderfolgenden Sonntagen werden sie über die betreffende Stelle gerollt. Viele der Kranken sind Moslems. (Riziq)

30 Taxi Nr. 16 hat zwei blaue Augen als Schutz gegen das Böse Auge auf der Motorhaube geklebt. Über den Augen steht: 'Gott ist groß' *(Allahu akbar)*. (Sohag)

31 Ein Bus trägt die etwas ungewöhnliche Hand (von Fatima?) und blaue Augen gegen das Böse Auge. (Karnak)

32 Der Eisverkäufer 'Id 'Abbas geht kein Risiko ein: Er stellt die Hand von Fatima zur Schau, die Nummer 5 in zwei Anordnungen, die sich auf ihre Finger beziehen, ein blaues Auge und '*Allahu akbar*.'(Kairo, *moulid* von Ahmad al-Rifa'i)

33 Eine Schaukel ist mit der Hand von Fatima geschützt. Auf dem Spanntuch steht das moslemische Glaubensbekenntnis: 'Es gibt nur einen Gott; Mohammed ist der Bote Gottes': *La ilaha illa 'llah, Muhammad rasoul Allah*. (Alexandria)

34 Neben dem Stadttor aus dem 11. Jahrhundert von Bab al-Futouh haben Derwische ein Zelt für die *moulid* von Sidi 'Ali al-Bayoumi aufgebaut. Das Minarett gehört zur Moschee von al-Hakim bi-Amr Allah. (Kairo)

35 Zwei Derwische vergnügen sich bei einem *zikr* des Dayfiya Ordens, morgens um halb zehn während der *moulid* von Abul Hasan al-Shazli. (Wadi Humaysara)

FRAUEN

36 Eine Dame trotzt dem Verkehr auf dem Tal'at Harb Platz, dem früheren Suleiman Pascha-Platz im Zentrum von Kairo.

37 Eine Bäuerin trinkt ein Glas Tee während der *moulid* auf dem Khanka Friedhof in der Nähe von Kairo. Auf diesem Friedhof liegen die Schreine von sechs oder sieben Heiligen, die alle vor weniger als zwanzig Jahren gestorben sind.

38 Während einer Prozession wartet eine koptische Frau darauf, daß die Ikone des heiligen Georg vorbeizieht. (Riziq)

39 Mädchen auf einer Schaukel in Bulaq, bei der *moulid* von al-Sultan Abul 'Ela. Der Eigentümer hilft einem Mädchen, sich zu überschlagen. Auf dem Querbalken ist die Hand von Fatima zu sehen, die vor Unfällen schützen soll. (Kairo)

40 Ein Mädchen verkauft Limonade und Tamarinde bei der christlichen *moulid* der heiligen Damiana in der Nähe von Mansoura. (Belqas)

41 Ein 'Ababda Mädchen füllt eine lederne Wassertasche an einer seichten Quelle. An diesem Morgen waren wir auf der Suche nach den Ruinen einer römischen Stadt im gebirgigen Hinterland von Berenice am Roten Meer. Ein Stück mit dem Land Rover, den Rest zu Fuß mit einem Führer. Am Ende einer engen Schlucht gingen wir nach rechts, und da saß sie mit ihrem Vater, ein paar Kamelen und vielen Ziegen. Die einzigen Lebewesen im Umkreis von Kilometern. (Shenshef)

42 Schwaden von Weihrauch umgeben eine Verkäuferin während der *moulid* der Sayyida Zaynab. Größere *moulid*s wie diese haben auch wirtschaftlichen Nutzen. Nicht nur Weihrauch, Rosenkränze und Koran-Bücher werden verkauft, sondern auch Töpfe, Pfannen, Spielzeug, Stoffe und große Mengen an Lebensmitteln und Getränken. (Kairo)

43 Eine Königin - ihre Hand berührt die Wade ihres Gatten

Pharao Amenhoteb III. - steht im Tempel von Luxor. Dadurch, daß sie bis vor sechzig Jahren im Sand begraben war, ist sie trotz ihrer dreitausend Jahre noch sehr gut erhalten. 1959 habe ich mich in diese kleine Statue verliebt und sie seitdem jedes Mal, wenn ich wieder in Luxor war, besucht.

44 Rote Zuckerpuppen werden bei der *moulid* von Abul Haggag in Luxor verkauft. Diese Form ist typisch für Oberägypten. In Kairo wickelt man zum Geburtstag des Propheten Zuckerpuppen in buntes Papier. (Luxor)

45 Die Göttin Hathor wird auf einer Säule des ptolemäischen Tempels von Kom Ombo dargestellt.

DIE PILGERFAHRT NACH MEKKA

46 Das Haus von *al-Hāgg* Zaki Fouli 'Abdel Galil und *al-Hāgga*, seiner Frau. Auf der Wand steht: 'Jeder, der mein Grab besucht, hat Recht auf meine Fürsprache' und 'Pilgerfahrt vollbracht, Sünden vergeben.' Gemalt 1975. (Danfiq, Westufer zwischen Qurna und Ballas)

47 Pilger auf dem Heimweg von Mekka werden in ihrem Dorfe irgendwo in Oberägypten begrüßt. Sie sitzen in Taxis, hinter der ausgelassenen Prozession.

48 Das Haus von *al-Hāgg* Mahmoud Farhat, verziert von einem Maler der Stadt Fayoum. Der Text lautet: 'Der Prophet hat gesagt: "Jeder, der mein Grab besucht, hat recht auf meine Fürsprache."' Datum: 20.9.1983. (I'lam, Fayoum)

49 Das Haus von *al-Hāgga* Badi'a 'Abdel Wahhab, die 1984 nach Mekka pilgerte. Neben der Tür stehen die Namen der vier gerechten Kalifen: Abu Bakr, 'Umar, 'Uthman und 'Ali. Über der Tür und den Fenstern stehen der Name der *hāgga* und das Datum ihrer Pilgerfahrt, dazu noch einige von Gottes neunundneunzig 'schönsten Namen': 'Er ist Gott, es gibt keinen Gott außer Ihm, der Gnädige, der Mitleidige, der König, der Heiligste, der Spender der Sicherheit, der Beschützer, der Erwecker des Vertrauens, der Glorreiche, der Allmächtige, der Größte, der Schöpfer, der Gestalter ...' (Amarna)

50 Das Haus von *al-Hāgg* Kamal, Sohn des *al-Hāgg* 'Abdel Sami' Isma'il, gemalt von 'Ali Sayyid, der zu der Zeit in den Sechzigern war. Kamal besuchte Mekka 1986. Typisch für das Werk von 'Ali Sayyid ist Buraq, das Pferd mit dem menschlichen Gesicht, das den Propheten auf seiner Reise

von Jerusalem in den Himmel trug. Wir sehen auch die Moschee des Grabs des Propheten in Medina, eine Kanzel *(minbar)*, die Texte, die bei Nr. 46 zitiert werden, 'Erfolg geschieht nur durch Gott', 'Die *hagg* ist die erlauchteste Belohnung', *'Allahu akbar'* und aus dem Koran: 'Sage: Gott ist der Herr.' (Ballas/Al-Mahrousa)

51 Wandmalerei von *'Id Yasin 'Ali*. Links: 'Der Vollmond ist über uns aufgegangen' (die Tage der 'weißen Nächte', wenn der Mond voll ist, in der Mitte des moslemischen Monats, enthalten besonders viel *baraka*), mit einem Sänger von religiösen Liedern und seinen Zuhörern; in der Mitte: 'Zu Deinen Diensten, o Gott' und rechts: *'Hagg* vollbracht, Sünden vergeben.' (Silwa Bahari)

52 Verblassendes Gemälde. (Shidmoh, Fayoum)

53 Wandmalerei auf dem Haus des *al-Hāgg 'Abdel Mawgoud* Mayhoub, der im Jahre 1982 Mekka besuchte. (Itsa, Fayoum)

54 Das Schiff, auf dem die Reise nach Mekka gemacht wurde. (Ma'goun, Fayoum)

55 Schiff in Minya al-Hayt, Fayoum.

FISCHE UND SCHIFFE

56 Diese Fischer kamen am frühen Morgen in Faraskour an, nachdem sie die ganze Nacht in der Lagune gefischt hatten. Sie verkaufen ihren Fang an Zwischenhändler, die ihn wiederum auf dem Markt von Damietta weiterverkaufen. Einige Teehäuser am Ufer waren schon geöffnet. (Faraskour)

57 Fischerboote liegen am Ufer des Qaroun See in Fayoum. Dieser Salzsee, der in einer Vertiefung unter dem Meeresspiegel liegt, erhält sein Wasser von einem Nebenfluß des Nils, dem Bahr Yousef, der die Oase von Fayoum bewässert. Er ist voller Fische, die als Fischbrut aus dem Mittelmeer hier ausgesetzt wurden. (Shakshouk)

58 Holzboote am Ufer des Roten Meeres. Ich weiß nicht, ob und zu welchem Zweck sie noch benutzt werden. (Qusayr)

59 Segelbarkassen entladen Steine in Esna. In den sechziger Jahren waren der Nil und die befahrbaren Kanäle voll mit diesen Schiffen. Jetzt benutzt man sie meistens zum Transport von Steinen und Ziegelsteinen auf bestimmten Abschnitten

des Flusses. Den verbleibenden Rest übernehmen Lastwagen. (Esna)

60 Köpfe kleiner Haie am Strand von Dahab am Golf von Akaba. (Dahab, Sinai)

61 Holzboote am gleichen Ort wie die auf Nr. 58 abgebildeten.

62 Das Fisch-Restaurant von *al-Hāgg* Hasan Mahmoud Abu Tahoun rüstet sich zur *moulid* von Sidi Ibrahim al-Desouqi. Innen ein Zitat aus dem Koran: 'Und Wir machten aus Wasser alles, was lebt.' (Desouq)

63 Seejungfrau und Wassergeist verzieren die 'Nil Fisch-Firma', etwas außerhalb von Kom Ombo auf der Autobahn nach Assuan.

TRANSPORT

64 Ein Bahnübergang bei Kafr al-Sheikh, im nördlichen Teil des Deltas. Der Zug läuft ein. Auf einem Pfahl im Hintergrund stehen die Namen von Ärzten, Zahnärzten und Rechtsanwälten, wie es in den kleinen Provinzstädten üblich ist. (Kafr al-Sheikh)

65 Der *'turmāy'*, die Straßenbahn. Diese, die Nummer 4163, fährt nach Matariya. Nach und nach werden die Straßenbahnen durch Busse ersetzt. (Kairo)

66 Der neue Besitzer eines Kamels versucht vergeblich, es in seinen Lastwagen zu kriegen. Kamele sind von Natur aus widerspenstige Tiere, und besonders nach den Strapazen der langen Reise zum Markt von Embaba. Ein einmonatiger Fußmarsch vom Sudan aus, die Überquerung des Nil bei Draw mit der Fähre, die Zug- oder Lastwagenfahrt von Draw bis Kairo - verständlicherweise haben sie danach keine Lust mehr zu einer weiteren Fahrt. (Embaba, Kairo)

67 Mustafa, unser Fahrer, hatte einen Vetter in einem Dorf am Ostufer, südlich von Asiut. Wir besuchten ihn auf unserem Weg in den tiefen Süden. Das Dorf entpuppte sich als Schauplatz von Taxis aus den frühen vierziger Jahren. Dies war unsere erste Begegnung mit dem Phänomen der Oldtimer-Taxis, die sich meist an solchen Orten konzentrieren, wo sich Werkstätten für die einzelnen Autotypen befinden. Im allgemeinen ersetzt ein robuster jugoslawischer Diesel den ursprünglichen Motor. Diese Autos sieht man hauptsächlich auf dem Land. Sie bilden eine mehr

oder weniger reguläre Verbindung, zum Beispiel zwischen Baba und al-Feshn, südlich von Beni Sueif. Auch dort sehen wir meistens amerikanische Autos aus den frühen vierziger Jahren. Ford von 1946 und 47 (Nr. 30) tun ihren Dienst weiter südlich, in Sohag. Tema kann sich eines der ersten stromlinienförmigen Studebaker rühmen. (Sahel Selim)

68 Vor langer Zeit war dieser Chevrolet Bel-Air (Beheira-Taxi Nr. 3222) der Privatwagen des berühmten Sängers Farid al-Atrash. Der Mann, der sich darüber beugt, ist der Wächter des Taxistandes. (Ityāy al-Baroud)

69 Im Dorf der blauen Chevrolet in der Provinz Kafr al-Sheikh erregte der Fotoapparat die übliche Heiterkeit. Diese Autos erinnerten mich an den grauen Chevrolet, den mein Vater 1947 kaufte, als es nur wenige Autos in den Niederlanden gab. Ich war darauf sehr stolz. Eines der Autos trägt die Inschrift *'Allahu akbar.'*

70 Ein Auto transportiert *zirs*, Tonkrüge, die das Wasser kühl halten, zwischen Assuan und Luxor. Diese Gefäße wurden bis vor kurzem hauptsächlich auf schwer beladenen, nilabwärts fahrenden Barkassen transportiert.

71 Abu Khalid verläßt Kairo mit seinem Karren in Richtung Süden. Der Text lautet: 'Ich vertraue auf Gott. Geh' in Frieden, Abu Khalid.' (Giza)

GEBÄUDE

72 Die nördliche Stadtmauer des mittelalterlichen Kairo in der Nähe von Bab al-Nasr, an einem frühen Morgen. Auf der rechten Seite erstrecken sich ausgedehnte Friedhöfe. Das Minarett ist das gleiche wie in Nr. 34. (Kairo)

73 Häuser in der Nähe des Bahnhofs von Sohag. Das rechte Gebäude beherbergt das Hotel Sohag sowie - gemäß den Namensschildern - die Rechtsanwälte Gamal Hasan, Muhammad Yousef 'Abdel Latif, 'Ala' al-Tarabishi, Ahmad Shawqi Mahmoud, Muhammad Mustafa und Mustafa Ibrahim, ein Ingenieurbüro und einen Steuerberater.

74 Das aus dem 4. Jahrhundert stammende Kloster des Heiligen Georg *(Mari Girgis)* al-Hadidi liegt im koptischen Dorf von Mari Girgis, in der Nähe von Akhmim. Es war lange Zeit unbewohnt, aber nach der Restaurierung von 1987 zogen drei Mönche aus dem St. Samuel-Kloster *(Amba Samwil)* in der Nähe von Minya ein. Eine Gruppe koptischer Kinder aus Sohag war dort bei einem Besuch. Nur wenige

Kilometer entfernt liegen die drei alten Klöster al-Shuhada', al-'Adhra und al-Mallak. (Mari Girgis)

75   Eine rot und blau bemalte Gebetsstelle *(masgid)* im Freien, in der Nähe von Nag' Hamadi. Es gab mehrere dieser *masgids* im Umkreis von wenigen Quadratkilometern.

76   Diese Moschee befindet sich auf halbem Weg zwischen Marsa Matrouh und der Oase von Siwa, in Bir al-Nuss (Quelle auf halbem Weg). Die Öltonne ist mit Wasser für die rituellen Waschungen gefüllt.

77   Der 'Supermarkt' von Husayn Sultan befindet sich an der Mittelmeerküste, westlich von Alexandria.

78   Haydars Geschäft am Strand von 'Agami in der Nähe von Alexandria ist im Winter geschlossen. Der Text lautet: *'Allahu akbar.'*

INSCHRIFTEN

79   Die Wiederherstellung der Demokratie in den achtziger Jahren brachte eine Fülle von Wahlplakaten hervor. Die besten wurden von der al-Wafd entworfen, einer Partei, die rechts von der Mitte steht und in der ersten Hälfte dieses Jahrhunderts eine wichtige Rolle spielte. Nasser verbot sie, aber jetzt ist sie wieder zugelassen. 'Al-Wafd ist die Hoffnung' verkündet dieses Plakat, das eine Frau zeigt, die Ägypten verkörpern soll. Sie lehnt sich ans Parlamentgebäude. Hinter dem Zaun wurde ein neues Kanalisationssystem gebaut, ein gigantisches Unternehmen, das große Teile der Stadt in ein noch größeres Chaos als gewöhnlich verwandelte. Die Spiegel wurden von einem Mann verkauft, der diese Stelle für die Dauer der *moulid* von Sayyida Zaynab besetzte. (Kairo)

80   'Wählt Wafd!' steht auf dem Plakat zur Linken, das das Emblem der Partei zeigt. Das rechte sagt: 'Die Wafd ist die Zukunft' und illustriert das mit den Porträts von Saad Zaghlul und Nahhas Pasha, die schon lange tot sind, und dem Parteichef Sarrag al-Din, der zu der Zeit über achtzig war. In der unteren rechten Ecke propagieren Minarette und Kirchtürme die al-Wafd als eine Partei für alle Religionen. (Kairo)

81   Koptische Christen haben hinter dem Kloster der heiligen Katharina Kreuze und das Christus-Monogramm ICXC auf der Spitze des Moses-Berges in Sinai eingraviert.

82   Anhänger des Rifa'i Scheichs Fathi Hasan Abu Shousha aus Minshat Bakhati im Bezirk Shibin al-Kom, Menoufiya, kündigen ihre Anwesenheit im Zelt an der rechten Seite an, während der *moulid* von Abul 'Abbas al-Mursi. In den Ecken stehen die Namen der ersten Kalifen. (Alexandria)

83   Nahe den alten Granitsteinbrüchen in Wada Hamamat, in den Bergen entlang des Roten Meeres, auf der Straße zwischen Qift und Qusayr, ist diese Kartusche von Ramses II. eine der vielen Inschriften aus der pharaonischen und griechisch-römischen Zeit.

84   Der Assuan-Staudamm wurde in den sechziger Jahren von den Russen gebaut. Eine Gedenktafel am Monument auf dem Damm trägt die Inschrift auf arabisch und russisch: 'Lange Jahre der vereinten Arbeit haben ein Denkmal arabisch-sowjetischer Freundschaft errichtet, das in seinem symbolischen Wert nicht weniger wichtig ist als das Monument des Staudamms selbst. Gamal Abdel Nasser.' Und in den Ecken steht: 'Der Staudamm ist eine Schlacht, die in einem Sieg resultierte, und dieser Sieg ist der Sieg von freien Menschen... der Sieg des Willens... der Sieg organisierter wissenschaftlicher Anstrengung, ... der Sieg der großen arabisch-russischen Freundschaft und der Sieg der Freiheit, des Friedens und des Fortschritts. Anwar al-Sadat.' Kurz nachdem dieser Text geschrieben wurde, mußten die Sowjets unter Schimpf und Schande Ägypten verlassen.
Das Porträt von Sadat und der Text sind offensichtlich erst nach der Fertigstellung des Monuments hinzugefügt worden, ungefähr so, wie sich der Pharao Ramses die Statue von Amenhoteb aneignete (Nr. 13). (Assuan)

85   Bei der *moulid* der heiligen Damiana im Delta nahe Mansoura trägt der Süßwarenverkäufer Girgis Shawqi Butros ein Plakat mit seinem Schutzheiligen *Mari Girgis*. Auf dem Schild steht eine Liste christlicher *moulids*, bei denen Girgis seine Süßigkeiten verkauft: St. Damiana, Mari Girgis in Kafr al-Dawar, der Heiligen Jungfrau in Mostorod nahe Kairo, Mari Girgis in Mit Damsis, St. Barsoum der Nackte und St. Theresa nahe Assiut. (Belqas)

WÜSTE UND OASEN

86   In Bir Murr (Die bittere Quelle) hängt ein Sack aus Ziegenleder, der mit Wasser gefüllt ist. Im Hintergrund liegt das Rote Meer. (Berenice)

87   Mitglieder des 'Ababda-Stammes haben ihre Habe außer Reichweite der Ziegen in den Baum gehängt, in einem *Wadi*

am Fuß des Pentedactylus-Berges, nicht weit von der sudanesischen Grenze an der Küste des Roten Meeres entfernt. Die Sonne ging gerade unter, und wir gingen unter den wachsamen Blicken einiger Soldaten in unser nahe gelegenes Lager. Wir befanden uns auf militärischem Gebiet.

88   Eine Oase im Meer: Mangroven vor der Küste des Roten Meeres zwischen Marsa 'Alam und Berenice.

89   Steinformationen wie Eisberge, nördlich der Oase von Farafra.

90   Granitbrocken im Ersten Katarakt, ein Stück flußaufwärts nach Assuan. In diesem Gebiet reicht die Wüste bis an den Nil.

91   In der Nähe der Inschriften zwischen Qift und Qusayr (Nr. 83) gibt es einen alten ägyptischen Sarkophag, der an dieser Stelle ausgehauen, zerbrochen und verlassen daliegt. Den Granit aus diesen Steinbrüchen rollte man früher auf Holzbalken an den Nil; eine Entfernung von fast hundert Kilometern. Dann wurde er auf Booten flußabwärts transportiert.

92   Im Dorf al-Qasr in der Oase Dakhla erinnert die Form der örtlichen Keramik an Unterseeboote.

93   Haus eines *hägg* in der Oase von Farafra.

GRÄBER

94   Sidi Nassar erhielt seinen Schrein 1981, weil er einer alten Frau im Traum erschienen war. Mehr ist über ihn nicht bekannt. Während der Errichtung fand man vierzig Schädel, die man im *maqam* beisetzte. (Kinayyiset al-Dahriya)

95   Drei der neununddreißig heiligen Gräber im Dorf Kinayyiset al-Dahriya, im nordwestlichen Delta. Das nächste ist das von Sidi Hamouda. Zwischen den Palmen im Hintergrund liegt Sidi Nassar, und rechts Sheikh Ahmad al-Zekayri. Im Dorf gibt es ebenfalls einen heiligen *gemayza*-Baum, Sidi Khadr genannt. Man hofft, daß noch ein Heiliger im Dorf erscheinen wird, um die magische Zahl 40 zu vervollständigen.

96   Gräber aus ungebrannten Ziegeln *(toub akhdar)* nahe Ashmunayn, in der Gegend von Minya. Obwohl einige der Gräber mit einer Kuppel versehen sind, ruhen in ihnen keine Heiligen.

97 *Déjeuner sur l'herbe* auf dem Khanka Friedhof während einer der zahlreichen *moulid*s, die man dort feiert.

98 Das Grabmal von Sheikh Zayed in Kafr al-'Arab, zwischen Birma und Basyoun im Delta. Die Gräber von Heiligen haben fast immer eine Kuppel. Einige der heiligen Gräber der Moslems befinden sich an Stellen, an denen früher ein christlicher Heiliger und noch früher eine pharaonische Gottheit verehrt wurden. Bei den Bäumen handelt es sich um Bergahorn, *gemayza*, die seit der Antike mit heiligen Stellen in Verbindung gebracht werden.

99 Auf einem bemalten Grab in Halfa Bahari, nicht weit von Nag' Hamadi, erinnert ein Rosenkranz, Wasserpfeife, Kaffee- oder Teekanne und Regenschirm an den Toten. Nirgendwo anders in Ägypten habe ich Gräber gesehen, die auf diese Art bemalt waren.

100 Mitten in Assiut liegt das Grab von Sheikh 'Ali 'Abdel Da'im 'Ali, der 1967 starb. Die *zirs* bieten den Durstigen Wasser.

101 'Ababda-Gräber an der Küste des Roten Meeres zwischen Marsa 'Alam und Berenice. Besucher hinterlassen eine Flagge.

A *saqiya*.
Une *saqiya*.
Eine *saqiya*.
(Sohag, 1959)

In November 1990, I returned to Egypt for a week, after an absence of two and a half years. Cairo had acquired another half million or so inhabitants, but was as entertaining as ever. At night I walked the Darb al-Ahmar with my old friend Raouf, chatted with those around, drank tea, and smoked a shisha.

Someone who had recently joined the embassy told me he had discovered a rural area just outside the city. The last morning of my visit, he fetched me from the hotel in Cairo at seven. There was no wind, and the city was covered by a thick blanket of smoke and dust. The sun was low and yellow. We drove to the southern suburb of Maadi, saw the high apartment blocks along the Nile, and left the car at the ferry, which took us to the other side. There, we crossed a highway, descended into a village already swallowed up by the city, and walked through it for ten minutes.

We crossed a canal, and came to another village. Here, there were high date palms between the houses. There was a Muslim holy tomb, and a little further ahead on the left-hand side we saw a small Coptic monastery with a number of domes. In the church mass was being read, and long tables covered with newspapers had been put outside, in the forecourt. Some visitors came in, who told us that today was the annual feast of the monastery's patron saints, Cosmas and Damian: *Qusmān wa-Damyān*.

Beyond the monastery there were two streets lined with Coptic tomb houses. Then we came to a cultivated area, irrigated by a maze of wide and narrow canals, from where the water was brought to the land by cows and donkeys walking in circles, moving big, creaking wheels. There was dust on the roads. The green land with its lanes, canals and date palms stretched from here until the desert fringe at Saqqara, ten or fifteen kilometres away, right next to the city of Cairo. The sky was clear, the silence perfect. The scenery could not have been very much different a thousand years ago.

It was half past eight now, and the farmers came out of the village riding their donkeys. They drove buffalo along, which had spent the night in the stables on the ground floors of the houses. Donkeys carried heavy bags with a mixture of the dung produced during the night and the sand that had been on the floor.

We walked for a while, and returned by way of the village. In a little shop opposite the Coptic tombs sufi music was played from a cassette. Children were walking by with iron slates on which the school master had written some words for them to study.

We crossed the highway, and took the ferry to Maadi. There I changed and boarded the metro, which took me to the centre of Cairo, just in time for an appointment at eleven at the Ministry of Foreign Affairs.

Après une absence de deux ans et demi, je suis retourné en Egypte pour une semaine en novembre 1990. Le Caire avait quelque demi-million d'habitants de plus, mais était divertissant comme toujours. La nuit je me promenais dans le quartier Darb al-Ahmar avec mon vieux ami Raouf, bavardais avec des gens que nous rencontrions, buvais un verre de thé et fumais une shisha.

Quelqu'un qui venait d'être attaché à l'ambassade me racontait qu'il avait découvert une zone rurale juste en dehors de la ville. Le dernier matin de mon séjour il vint me chercher à l'hôtel au Caire à sept heures. Il n'y avait pas de vent et la ville était enveloppée d'un nuage de fumée et de poussière. Le soleil était bas et jaune.

Nous roulâmes vers le faubourg sud de Maadi, vîmes les hauts immeubles à appartements le long du Nil et laissâmes la voiture à l'embarcadère du ferry-boat qui nous porta vers l'autre rive. Là nous traversâmes une route nationale, descendîmes dans un village déjà englouti par la ville, que nous traversâmes en dix minutes. Nous franchîmes un canal et arrivâmes à un autre village. Ici, il y avait entre les maisons de hauts palmiers dattiers. Il y avait une tombe sainte musulmane et un peu plus loin à gauche nous découvrîmes un petit monastère copte avec quelques dômes. Dans l'église on était en train de dire la messe et de longues tables couvertes de journaux avaient été mises dehors dans la cour. Quelques visiteurs entrèrent et nous racontèrent qu'aujourd'hui c'était la fête annuaire des patrons du monastère, Cosmas et Damien: *Qusmān wa-Damyān*.

Au-delà du monastère il y avait deux rues bordées de maisons funéraires coptes. Puis nous arrivâmes à une zone cultivée, irriguée par un dédale de canaux larges et étroits à partir desquels l'eau était transportée vers la terre par des vaches et des ânes qui tout en marchant dans un cercle mouvaient de grandes roues grinçantes. La route était poussiéreuse. La terre verte avec ses chemins, ses canaux et ses palmiers dattiers s'étendait devant nous jusqu'au bord du désert à Saqqarah, dix ou quinze kilomètres plus loin, tout près de la ville du Caire. Le ciel s'était dégagé, le silence était complet. Il y a mille ans la scène ne pouvait pas avoir été très différente.

Il était maintenant huit heures et demie et les fermiers quittaient le village avec leurs ânes. Ils poussaient des buffles, qui avaient passé la nuit dans les étables aux rez-de-chaussée des maisons. Des ânes portaient de lourds sacs contenant un mélange du fumier de la nuit et du sable qui se trouvait par terre.

Pendant quelque temps nous poursuivîmes notre promenade et puis nous retournâmes par le village. Dans une petite boutique en face des tombes coptes de la musique soufi jouée à une cassette se faisait entendre. Des enfants passaient avec des ardoises sur lesquels le maître d'école avait écrit quelques mots qu'ils devaient étudier.

Nous traversâmes la route nationale et prîmes le ferry-boat pour Maadi où je me changeai. Puis je pris le métro qui me porta au centre du Caire, juste à temps pour un rendez-vous à onze heures au Ministère des Affaires étrangères.

Im November 1990 kehrte ich für eine Woche nach Ägypten zurück, nach einer Abwesenheit von zweieinhalb Jahren. Kairo war wieder um eine halbe Million gewachsen, jedoch so unterhaltsam wie eh und je. Nachts spazierte ich mit meinem alten Freund Raouf durch die Darb al-Ahmar, führte Gespräche, trank Tee und rauchte eine shisha.

Ein Mitarbeiter der Botschaft, der erst seit kurzem in Kairo war, erzählte mir, daß er ein ländliches Gebiet direkt außerhalb der Stadt entdeckt habe. Am letzten Morgen meines Besuches holte er mich um sieben Uhr von meinem Hotel in Kairo ab. Es wehte kein Wind, und über der Stadt lag eine dicke Decke aus Smog und Staub. Die Sonne stand tief und gelb am Himmel. Wir fuhren in die südliche Vorstadt Maadi, sahen den hohen Wohnkomplex entlang des Nils und ließen das Auto bei dem Fährboot, das uns auf die andere Seite brachte. Dort überquerten wir die Autobahn, kamen in ein Dorf, das sich die Stadt schon einverleibt hatte, und durchquerten es innerhalb von zehn Minuten.

Wir überquerten einen Kanal und betraten ein anderes Dorf. Hier standen hohe Dattelpalmen zwischen den Häusern. Wir sahen ein heiliges moslemisches Grabmal und etwas weiter links ein kleines koptisches Kloster mit mehreren Kuppeln. In der Kirche wurde die Messe gelesen, und man hatte lange Tische, die mit Zeitungen bedeckt waren, in den Vorhof hinaus gestellt. Ein paar Besucher kamen und erzählten uns, daß am heutigen Tag das Fest der beiden Schutzheiligen des Klosters, Cosmas und Damian (*Qusmān wa-Damyān*), gefeiert werde.

Jenseits des Klosters lagen zwei Straßen, die koptische Grabmäler säumten. Dann gelangten wir in eine landwirtschaftlich kultivierte Gegend, für deren Bewässerung ein Labyrinth aus breiten und schmalen Kanälen sorgte. Von hier aus wurde das Wasser von Kühen und Eseln, die im Kreis liefen und schwere, knarrende Räder bewegten, aufs Land getragen. Die Straßen waren mit Staub bedeckt. Das grüne Land mit seinen Feldwegen, Kanälen und Dattelpalmen erstreckte sich zehn oder fünfzehn Kilometer weit von hier bis hin zum Wüstenrand bei Saqqara, unterhalb von Kairo. Der Himmel war klar, die Stille total. Vor tausend Jahren hätte diese Szene nicht viel anders aussehen können.

Es war inzwischen halb neun; die Bauern kamen auf ihren Eseln aus dem Dorf. Sie trieben Büffel mit sich, die die Nacht in den Ställen im Erdgeschoß ihrer Häuser verbracht hatten. Die Esel schleppten schwere Taschen mit einer Mischung aus dem Dünger, den sie in der Nacht produziert hatten, und dem Sand, der den Fußboden bedeckte.

Wir spazierten eine Weile umher und kehrten über den Dorfweg wieder zurück. In einem kleinen Geschäft gegenüber den koptischen Grabmälern ertönte Sufi-Kassettenmusik. Kinder kamen mit Eisentafeln vorbei, auf die der Lehrer einige Worte zum Lernen geschrieben hatte.

Wir überquerten die Autobahn und kehrten per Fährboot nach Maadi. Dort zog ich mich um und nahm die Metro in die Stadtmitte von Kairo, wo ich gerade noch rechtzeitig um elf Uhr zu einem Termin im Außenministerium kam.

abu father (of)

Allahu akbar God is most great

baraka blessing

bir well

gallabiya the garment worn by Egyptian peasants

gemayza sycamore tree

hagg the Mecca pilgrimage

hāgg Mecca pilgrim (male)

hāgga id. (female)

higab amulet

khamsa five

koshari mixture of rice, macaroni and lentils

maqam shrine

mari saint (Coptic)

masgid place for prayer

mawlid birthday festival

minbar pulpit

mirmah horse race

mizmar a wind instrument

moulid see *mawlid*

nabi prophet

qarabni a church servant

qurban holy bread (Coptic)

rababa a single-stringed violin

saha holy tomb with mosque and facilities for visitors

salakhana slaughterhouse

saqiya a well actuated by an animal

shafa'a intercession

sheikh elderly, venerable or holy man

sheikha id. (female)

shisha a water pipe standing on the ground

tahtib Upper Egyptian stick dance

tawassut mediation

toub akhdar adobe; unbaked bricks

wadi a valley

yawm 'Arafat one of the days of the hagg

zabiba raisin or sultana; a callosity on the
forehead caused by frequent praying

zikr remembrance (of God); a mystic dance

zir earthen water vessel

I have tried to render the Arabic words optically in as simple a manner as possible. Unless there was a probability of mispronunciation (turmāy, Ityāy), or a semantic distinction (hagg meaning pilgrimage, hāgg a pilgrim), I have refrained from using ā and ī to indicate long vowels. The long stressed u is written ou.

Likewise, diacritical dots have been omitted. D stands for d and ḍ, h for h and ḥ, s for s, ṣ and sometimes th, z for z, ẓ and dh.

G denotes a sound which in classical Arabic is pronounced like j in 'jam', but which in Cairo is g like 'go'. Thus the reader is free to pronounce hagg or Abul Haggag in the classical or Upper Egyptian way, i.e., hajj or Abul Hajjaj.

Likewise, q will, depending on whether the speaker is a Cairene or an Upper Egyptian, be pronounced either as a glottal stop or as g in 'go'. The city of Qena is known in Cairo as Ena, and as Gena in Qena itself. Kh sounds like ch in German 'ach'.

In place names, personal names and familiar words, I have kept the usual spelling as far as there is one: Esna, Luxor, sheikh, etc.

abu père (de)

Allahu akbar Dieu est infiniment grand

baraka bénédiction

bir puits

cheikh vieillard, homme vénérable ou saint

cheikha femme vénérable ou sainte

gallabiya habit

gemayza sycamore

hagg le pèlerinage à La Mecque

hāgg pèlerin de La Mecque

hāgga pèlerine de La Mecque

higab amulette

khamsa cinq

koshari mélange de riz, macaroni et lentilles

maqam tombe sainte

mari saint (copte)

masgid lieu de prière

mawlid fête d'anniversaire

minbar chaire

mirmah course de chevaux

mizmar instrument à vent

moulid voyez *mawlid*

nabi prophète

qarabni serviteur d'église

qurban pain saint (copte)

rababa violon à une seule corde

saha tombe sainte avec mosquée et équipée pour des visiteurs

salakhana abattoir

saqiya puits actionné par un animal

shafa'a intercession

shisha narguilé qui se pose par terre

tahtib danse à bâton de Haute-Egypte

tawassut médiation

toub akhdar adobe; brique crue

yawm 'Arafat un des jours du hagg

zabiba raisin sec ou raisin sultana; une callosité sur
    le front qui se forme par la prière fréquente

zikr commémoration (de Dieu); une danse mystique

zir récipient à eau en terre cuite

J'ai essayé de rendre les mots arabes du point de vue optique le plus simplement possible. A moins qu'il n'y ait la possibilité d'une mauvaise prononciation (turmāy, Ityāy) ou qu'il s'agisse d'une distinction sémantique (hagg qui signifie pèlerinage et hāgg qui signifie pèlerin), j'ai renoncé à utiliser ā et ī pour indiquer des voyelles longues ; u se prononce comme ou dans tout et ou indique la longue voyelle tonique ou.

De la même manière les points diacritiques ont été omis. D représente d et ḍ, h représente h et ḥ, s représente s, ṣ et parfois th, z représente z, ẓ et dh.

G représente un son qui se prononce en arabe classique comme dj dans 'adjudant', mais qui se prononce au Caire comme g dans 'godet'. Pour prononcer hagg ou Abul Haggag le lecteur a donc le choix entre la manière du Caire, et la manière dont ces mots se prononcent dans la Haute-Egypte et en arabe classique, c'est-à-dire hadjdj ou Abul Hadjdjadj.

De la même façon, selon que le locuteur est originaire du Caire ou de la Haut-Egypte, le q se prononce soit comme une occlusive glottique soit comme le g de 'godet'. Au Caire la ville de Qena est donc connue comme Ena, mais à Qena elle-même comme Guena.

Kh a une consonance comme ch dans l''ach' allemand.

Pour les noms des lieux, des personnes et des mots familiers je me suis tenu à l'orthographe habituelle s'il y en a une: Esna, Louxor, cheikh, et cetera.

abu Vater (von)

Allahu akbar Gott ist groß

baraka Segen

bir Brunnen

gallabiya Gewand

gemayza Ahornbaum

hagg Pilgerfahrt nach Mekka

hāgg Mekka Pilger (männlich)

hāgga Mekka Pilger (weiblich)

higab Amulett

khamsa fünf

koshari Mischung aus Reis, Makkaroni und Linsen

maqam Schrein

mari (koptischer Heiliger)

masgid Gebetsplatz

mawlid Geburtstagsfestival

minbar Kanzel

mirmah Pferderennen

mizmar ein Windinstrument

moulid siehe *mawlid*

nabi Prophet

qarabni ein Kirchendiener

qurban heiliges (koptisches) Brot

rababa einsaitige Geige

saha heiliges Grabmal mit einer Moschee und Einrichtungen für Besucher

salakhana Schlachthaus

saqiya eine Quelle, die von einem Tier bedient wird

shafa'a Fürsprache

sheikh älterer, ehrwürdiger oder heiliger Mann

sheikha idem (weiblich)

shisha Wasserpfeife, die auf dem Boden steht

tahtib oberägyptischer Stocktanz

tawassut Vermittlung

toub akhdar Adobe; ungebrannter Lehmziegel

wadi ein Tal

yawm 'Arafat einer der Tage der hagg

zabiba Rosine; eine Schwiele auf der Stirn, verursacht durch
   häufiges Beten

zikr Erinnerung (an Gott); mystischer Tanz

zir irdenes Wassergefäß

Ich habe versucht, die arabischen Wörter optisch so einfach wie möglich zu übertragen. Außer dem Fall wo eine Möglichkeit der falschen Aussprache bestand, wie bei turmāy, Ityāy, oder eine semantische Unterscheidung (hagg bedeutet Pilgerfahrt, hāgg ein Pilger), habe ich es unterlassen, ein ā und ī zu benutzen, um lange Vokale anzudeuten. Das lange betonte u wird ou geschrieben.

Ebenso habe ich die diakritischen Punkte weggelassen. D steht für d und ḍ, h für h und ḥ, s für s, ṣ und manchmal th, z für z, ẓ und dh.

G bezeichnet einen Klang, der im klassischen Arabisch wie dsch ausgesprochen wird, in Kairo jedoch wie in gehen. So bleibt es dem Leser überlassen, hagg oder Abul Haggag in der klassischen oder oberägyptischen Aussprache auszusprechen, also hadsch oder Abul Hadschadsch.

Ebenso wird q – abhängig ob der Sprecher aus Kairo oder Oberägypten ist – ausgesprochen wie ein Knacklaut oder wie g in gehen. Die Stadt Qena ist in Kairo bekannt als Ena und in Qena selbst als Gena. S wird immer wie in essen ausgesprochen und z wie s in See. Kh klingt wie ch im deutschen ach.

Bei Ortsnamen, Personennamen und familiären Wörtern habe ich die gebräuchliche Schreibweise, sofern es eine überhaupt gibt, übernommen: Esna, Luxor, Scheich, Suk usw.

Copyright © 1992 by Nicolaas Biegman/The Goose Press

All rights reserved. No part of this publication may be reproduced or transmitted in any form or by any means, electronic or mechanical including photocopy, recording or any information storage and retrieval system without prior permission in writing from the publisher.

Co-ordination Harry Kraaij
Translation Helga Marx (G), Bureau Jenny Spits (F)
Text editing Kist & Kilian, H.J. Scheepmaker
Design Irma Boom
Production Gorenjski Tisk, Kranj
Printed and *bound* in Slovenia

First published in Great Britain in 1992 by Thames and Hudson Limited, London by arrangement with The Goose Press, Amsterdam.

ISBN 0 500 97405 5 (Thames and Hudson, London)

Cover A barber on a bench at the *moulid* of Abu Misallam.

Couverture Un barbier sur un banc lors du *moulid* d'Abu Misallam.

Umschlag Ein Barbier auf einer Bank während der *moulid* von Abu Misallam.

(First published in N.H. Biegman, *Egypt - Moulids, Saints and Sufis*, Gary Schwartz/SDU and Kegan Paul International, 1990)

Back cover A sticker with the Hand of Fatima and a blue eye, made to protect a car or a bicycle from the Evil Eye.
The text written on the hand reads: 'The Eye has hit me, and the Lord of the Throne has rescued me.'
The second text reads: 'People, Evil, stop your envious prattle!'
On the reverse: stampato in Italia.

Plat verso Un auto-collant de la Main de Fatima avec un œil bleu, fait pour protéger une voiture ou une bicyclette contre le Mauvais Œil.
Le texte écrit sur la main veut dire: 'L'Œil m'a frappé et le Seigneur du Trône m'a sauvé.'
Le deuxième texte veut dire: 'Peuple, Malheur, arrêtez votre caquetage envieux!'
Au verso: stampato in Italia.

Hinterdeckel Ein Sticker mit der Hand von Fatima und einem blauen Auge, der Auto oder Fahrrad vor dem Bösen Auge schützen soll.
Der Text auf der Hand lautet: 'Das Auge hat mich getroffen, und der Herr des Thrones hat mich gerettet.'
Der zweite Text lautet: 'Menschen, Böse, hört auf mit eurem neidischen Geplapper!'
Auf der Rückseite steht: stampato in Italia.